Religious Proverbs

Religious Proverbs
Over 1600 Adages from 18 Faiths Worldwide

COMPILED BY
ALBERT KIRBY GRIFFIN

McFarland & Company, Inc., Publishers
Jefferson, North Carolina, and London

British Library Cataloguing-in-Publication data are available

Library of Congress Cataloguing-in-Publication Data

Griffin, Albert Kirby, 1963–
    Religious proverbs : over 1600 adages from 18 faiths worldwide /
compiled by Albert Kirby Griffin.
        p. cm.
    Includes bibliographical references and index.
    ISBN 0-89950-621-6 (lib. bdg.: 50# alk paper) ∞
        1. Religious life–Quotations, maxims, etc. 2. Sacred books–
Quotations, maxims, etc. 3. Proverbs. I. Title.
BL624.G738 1991
291.4′4–dc20   91-52616
                                                                CIP

Manufactured in the United States of America

McFarland & Company, Inc., Publishers
    Box 611, Jefferson, North Carolina 28640

This book is dedicated
to those who benefit from its wisdom

Contents

Acknowledgments   ix

Foreword   xi

The Proverbs

Action	1	God	61
Body	3	Golden Rule	67
Character	6	Good	69
Children	8	Greed	72
Conduct	9	Happiness	74
Death	12	Hatred	77
Decision	16	Heart	79
Deeds	18	Humility	82
Delusion	20	Judgment	86
Desire	23	Knowledge	89
Destiny	25	Language	92
Discipline	28	Leadership	96
Education	30	Love	99
Envy	33	Lust	102
Error	35	Mankind	105
Evil	38	Mind	109
Faith	40	Moderation	113
Falsehood	44	Paradox	116
Family	46	Perception	118
Fear	49	Possessions	121
Fool	51	Prayer	122
Forgiving	53	Quest	125
Friendship	55	Reward	130
Giving	57	Self	132

viii   CONTENTS

Senses	135	Unity	152
Service	137	Virtue	154
Sin	140	Wealth	156
Soul	142	Wisdom	158
Suffering	144	Work	162
Thought	146	World	164
Truth	148	Worship	166

Sources   169
Bibliography   189
Index by Religion and Source   193
Index by Key Words and Topics   199

Acknowledgments

This compilation would have not been possible had it not been for the wonderful support I received. I will forever be thankful to Mary Louise Rea and Louise Dauner for their experience and love. I am indebted to Professor Christian Kloesel for his time and his undying commitment. Additionally, I would like to thank the University of Chicago, Butler University, Indiana University, the Library of Congress, and Dean James East at Indiana University–Purdue University at Indianapolis for the use of their facilities.

On a personal level, I am blessed to have friends whom I will always love and cherish. I would like to thank my parents and grandmothers, who pointed me down a spiritual path; Vanessa Prestridge, who got the ball rolling; David and Kathy, whose suggestions greatly benefited my effort; Tom and Kristin Cunningham, Andy and Paige Hunkin, and Ted and Ida Kirby. Finally, I would like to thank Vibeke Rasmussen, Greg Cox, Mark and Vicki Adams, Craig Altmeyer, Steve and Lisa Pearcy, John and Kelly Huguenard, and Elena Schmunk.

Foreword

If a fool can see his own folly, he in this at least is wise, but
the fool who thinks he is wise, he indeed is the real fool.
Dhammapada 63 (Buddhism)

Do you see a man wise in his own eyes?
There is more hope for a fool than for him.
Proverbs 26.12 (Judaeo-Christian)

Recently, I read the Dhammapada, a Buddhist text containing
the sayings of the Buddha and reflecting quite a cache of teachings
and wisdom. Noticing some similarities between the Dhammapada
and the book of Proverbs in the Bible, I wondered if other religious
texts contained similar advice.

The utterance of God is a lamp, whose light is these words.
Gleanings from the Writings of
Baha'u'llah 288 (Baha'i)

All scripture is given by inspiration of God, and is profitable
for doctrine, for reproof, for correction, for instruction in
righteousness.
2 Timothy 3.16 (Christianity)

The answer to my question is reflected in the pages that follow.
I believe that most religions offer teachings that contribute posi-
tively to our lives. With the exception of the selections taken from
the inscriptions at the Shinto shrines, all proverbs included here are
from religious texts. Certainly all the wisdom that mankind has
amassed could not be collected in a single volume. Consequently,

this collection serves as a mere introduction to the religious wisdom that our forebears have formulated and left for us. There is, of course, no substitute for reading the original, complete texts.

> Systems of faith are different, but the Deity is one.
> Vemana's Padyamulu (Hinduism)

> Wherever ye be, hasten emulously after good.
> One day God will bring you all together.
> Koran 2.143 (Islam)

Just as the light from a star moves in an infinite number of directions, so do our lives move on an infinite number of spiritual paths. We share common experiences, but lead different lives: our spiritual lives should reflect those differences and commonalities.

> Keep these sayings in thy heart. Having listened to the truths laid down in the Scriptures, follow them duly.
> Mahabharata 12.103.50–51 (Hinduism)

> A sensible man will take a proverb to heart.
> Ecclesiasticus 3.29 (Judaeo-Christian)

Traditionally, the deity is portrayed as a masculine figure in most religious literature, and the generic reference to humanity seems usually to be masculine as well. The proverbs included in this book are of course equally applicable to men and women; it is in this spirit that I have chosen them.

> Heaven helps those who help themselves.
> I Ching 26.6 (Taoism)

> Seeker after the highest truth! Study the Sacred Lore, in order to cause yourself and others to attain perfection.
> Uttara-Dhyayana Sutra 11.32 (Jainism)

My motive in compiling the proverbs has been to illustrate that the essence of religious wisdom is universal. Although readers may differ on what is important or true, I hope that everyone will find at least something of value here.

As all have not faith, seek ye diligently and teach one another
words of wisdom; yea, seek ye out of the best books words
of wisdom; seek learning even by study and also by faith.
> Doctrine and Covenants 88.118
> (Mormonism)

The truest sayings are paradoxical.
> Tao Teh Ching 78 (Taoism)

I have chosen single-sentence proverbs for the most part and,
according to their theme and meaning, have placed them into sections bearing the appropriate title—even as some of the proverbs
might easily have found a home in several different other sections
as well. As a further aid to the reader, I provide a descriptive list
of the sources from which the proverbs were quoted.

Know that these teachings can satisfy your needs.
It is time to listen and to meditate on these words.
> Tibetan Book of the Dead (Buddhism)

Regard all men as equal,
Since God's light is contained in the heart of each.
> Hymns of Guru Nanak (Sikhism)

Our religions offer a wealth of teachings. By studying them, we
can take an immeasurable step toward spiritual fulfillment. Know
that we are brothers, divided and autonomous, but with the ability
and the power to become one with ourselves and with our God.

Gold and silver make a man stand firm,
but better still is good advice.
> Ecclesiasticus 40.25 (Judaeo-Christian)

Religion is good advice.
> Forty-Two Traditions of An-Nawawi (Islam)

A proverb is much matter decocted into few words.

Thomas Fuller

I am of the opinion that there are no proverbial sayings which are not true, because they are all sentences drawn from experience itself, who is the mother of all sciences.

Cervantes

General observations drawn from particulars are the jewels of knowledge, comprehending great store in a little room.

John Locke

The proverb condenses the meaning and power of a thousand words into one short and simple sentence, and it is the more effective because it carries so much force in so compact a form.

Daniel March

The wisdom of many and the wit of one.

Lord John Russell

The Proverbs

ACTION

1 The way to do is to be.
    Tao Teh Ching 47 (Taoism)

2 By one's actions one becomes.
    Uttara-Dhyayana Sutra 25.33 (Jainism)

3 A person is justified by what he does and not by faith alone.
    James 2.24 (Christianity)

4 Look to what you do,
       for that is what you are worth.
    The Song of the Dervish (Sufism)

5 It is not the knowing that is difficult, but the doing.
    Shu King 4.8 (Confucianism)

6 Make your acts your piety.
    Bhagavad Gita 2 (Hinduism)

7 Not inquiry but action is the chief thing.
    The Sayings of the Fathers 1.17 (Judaism)

8 Actions differ because the inspirations of the states of being differ.
    The Book of Wisdom 9 (Sufism)

1

9   The way to use life is to do nothing through acting,
    The way to use life is to do everything through being.
    Tao Teh Ching 37 (Taoism)

10 Let me act nobly in deed, word, and thought.
    Anguttara Nikaya 3.35.3 (Buddhism)

11 What you wish others to do, do yourself.
    The Sayings of Sri Ramakrishna (Hinduism)

12 Be persistent in good action.
    Hadith 218 (Islam)

13 Whenever our actions fail to produce the effect desired, we
    should look for the cause in ourselves.
    Mencius 4.1.4 (Confucianism)

14 The embodied soul alone does actions, it alone wanders in the
    long chain of mundane existence, it alone takes birth, it
    alone dies, and it alone enjoys the fruits of its actions.
    Twelve Meditations (Jainism)

15 Let all things be done decently and in order.
    1 Corinthians 14.40 (Christianity)

16 A man rises or goes down by his own actions:
    like the builder of a wall,
    or as the digger of a well.
    Hitopadesa (Hinduism)

17 Thy woe and weal are according to thine acts.
    Adi Granth (Sikhism)

18 Faced with what is right,
    to leave it undone shows a lack of courage.
    Analects II.24 (Confucianism)

19 Actions will be judged by their intentions.
    Hadith 1 (Islam)

20 By sincerity of acting
one will become pure in his actions.
Uttara-Dhyayana Sutra 29.52 (Jainism)

21 Action is greater than inaction:
perform therefore thy task in life.
Bhagavad Gita 3.8 (Hinduism)

22 If one is guided by profit in one's actions,
one will incur much ill will.
Analects IV.12 (Confucianism)

23 None of your oppressive acts are concealed and in secret.
The Book of Enoch 96.15 (Judaism)

24 Men's acts in this world shall bear witness in God's court.
Sloks of Shaikh Farid (Sikhism)

25 The Lord is a God of knowledge,
and by him actions are weighed.
1 Samuel 2.3 (Judaeo-Christian)

BODY

26 The spirit is willing, but the body is weak.
Matthew 26.41 (Christianity)

27 One who would walk in the Way of Truth
must close the eyes of the flesh
and open the eyes of the spirit.
Gorikai (Shinto)

28 All that belongs to the body (must be considered) as the
product of ignorance.
Knowledge of Spirit (Hinduism)

29   The body is the scabbard of the soul.
Talmud (Judaism)

30   The wise man regards the body as only an instrument through
the help of which, by meditating on the Truth and knowing
the one existence, he may become free.
Bhagavata Purana (Hinduism)

31   Fear not the flesh nor love it.
Gospel of Phillip II.66. 4–5 (Gnosticism)

32   The city of the body arises in its beauty;
and within it the palace of the mind has been built.
Songs of Kabir XCII (Sikhism)

33   Though my body is sick my mind shall not be sick.
Samyutta Nikaya 3.2 (Buddhism)

34   It is better for you to lose one part of your body than for your
whole body to go into hell.
Matthew 5.30 (Christianity)

35   Your body is not for your own freedom.
Gorikai (Shinto)

36   When he no longer thinks of the personal body as self neither
failure nor success can ail him.
Tao Teh Ching 13 (Taoism)

37   The Spirit gives life; the flesh means nothing.
John 6.63 (Christianity)

38   This human body is a theatre of pleasure and pain.
Garuda Purana (Hinduism)

39   Dost thou think thy body is a small thing,
while in thee is enfolded the universe?
Selections from the Writings
of 'Abdu'l Baha (Baha'i)

40   The body is not for fornication, but for the Lord.
                    1 Corinthians 6.13 (Christianity)

41   Of all the parts of a man's body there is none more excellent
     than the pupil of the eye.
                    Mencius 4.1.15 (Confucianism)

42   Put away all fear for this body.
                    Songs of Kabir LXIV (Sikhism)

43   If you persist and live in the body, you dwell in rusticity.
                    The Teachings
                    of Silvanus VII. 94.22–24 (Gnosticism)

44   Make your bellies hungry and your livers thirsty,
        and your bodies naked that perchance your hearts
        may see God in this world.
                    Hadith (Islam)

45   Keep your bodies as the temples of God.
                    The Epistle of Ignatius
                    to the Philadelphians 2.15 (Christianity)

46   If ye subdue the imperfections of your flesh,
        ye will think only of God.
                    Bani (Hinduism)

47   The physical body is the home.
                    Tan Ching 20 (Zen)

48   The body which thou deemest permanent is only a two-days
     guest.
                    Adi Granth (Sikhism)

49   How foolish to spend your lifetime without meaning when a
     precious human body is so rare a gift.
                    Mila Grubum (Buddhism)

50   See nothing; hear nothing;
        guard your spirit in quietude
        and your body will go right of its own accord.
                    Chuang-tzu (Taoism)

CHARACTER

51   Being good as a son and obedient as a young man is,
        perhaps, the root of a man's character.
                    Analects I.2 (Confucianism)

52   For each one by his deed and his knowledge will reveal his
        nature.
                    On the Origin
                    of the World II.127.16–17 (Gnosticism)

53   Be in peace in pleasure and pain, in gain and in loss, in victory
        or in the loss of a battle.
                    Bhagavad Gita 2.38 (Hinduism)

54   A man of benevolence never worries;
        a man of wisdom is never in two minds;
        a man of courage is never afraid.
                    Analects XIV.28 (Confucianism)

55   If you falter in times of trouble,
        how small is your strength!
                    Proverbs 24.10 (Judaeo-Christian)

56   The perfect man ignores self;
        the divine man ignores achievement;
        the true Sage ignores reputation.
                    Chuang-tzu (Taoism)

57   A gentleman who lacks gravity does not inspire awe.
                    Analects I.8 (Confucianism)

58 If you desire to obtain help from the Gods,
        put away pride
                    Oracle of the Gods of Kasuga (Shinto)

59 If you did not do so for the sake of riches,
        You must have done so for the sake of novelty.
                    Shih King (Confucianism)

60 The gentleman agrees with others without being an echo.
        The small man echoes without being in agreement.
                    Analects XIII.23 (Confucianism)

61 Even as a great rock is not shaken by the wind,
        the wise man is not shaken by praise or by blame.
                    Dhammapada 81 (Buddhism)

62 As a man is, so is his strength.
                    Judges 8.21 (Judaeo-Christian)

63 The man of honour thinks of his character,
        the inferior man thinks of his position.
                    Analects IV.11 (Confucianism)

64 If proudly honored, do not rejoice;
        And do not sorrow, if abused.
                    Mahabharata (Hinduism)

65 Men of good character and morals are easy to please.
                    Sutra-krit-anga II.2.75 (Jainism)

66 A man not tempted is not proved.
                    Logia (Christianity)

67 The superior man understands what is right;
        the inferior man understands what will sell.
                    Analects 7 (Confucianism)

68   Not to be cheered by praise,
        Not to be grieved by blame,
      But to know thoroughly one's own virtues or powers
        Are the characteristics of an excellent man.
                    Subhashita Ratna Nidhi (Buddhism)

69   Everyone is divinely furthered according to his character.
                    Hadith 359 (Islam)

70   The gentleman is troubled by his own lack of ability,
        not by the failure of others to appreciate him.
                    Analects XV.19 (Confucianism)

CHILDREN

71   A child he is, but he speaks like the old;
        No child do I deem him, but a man of age.
                    Mahabharata (Hinduism)

72   The wise hear and see as little children.
                    Tao Teh Ching 49 (Taoism)

73   The pupil must regain the child state he has lost ere the first
        sound can fall upon his ear.
                    The Voice of the Silence (Buddhism)

74   Unless you change and become like little children,
        you will never enter the kingdom of heaven.
                    Matthew 18.3 (Christianity)

75   Great men have the nature of children.
                    The Sayings of Sri Ramakrishna (Hinduism)

76   A youth is to be regarded with respect.
                    Analects IX (Confucianism)

77 A little child shall lead them.
>>>>>> Isaiah 11.6 (Judaeo-Christian)

78 Abandon thought and thinking and be just as a child.
>>>>>> Saraha's Treasury of Songs 57 (Buddhism)

79 Children are an adornment of the life of this world.
>>>>>> Koran 18.44 (Islam)

80 He who possesses virtue in all its solidity is like unto a little child.
>>>>>> Tao Teh Ching 55 (Taoism)

81 Forget all the worldly knowledge that thou hast
acquired and become ignorant as a child,
and then wilt thou get the divine wisdom.
>>>>>> The Sayings of Sri Ramakrishna (Hinduism)

82 The Spirit himself testifies with our spirit that we are God's children.
>>>>>> Romans 8.16 (Christianity)

83 He who has children is far above the childless man.
>>>>>> Avesta (Zoroastrianism)

84 Empty is the childless home.
>>>>>> Hitopadesa (Hinduism)

85 The great man is he who does not lose his child's heart.
>>>>>> Mencius 4.2.12 (Confucianism)

CONDUCT

86 Make it your guiding principle to do your best for others and to
be trustworthy in what you say.
>>>>>> Analects IX.25 (Confucianism)

87 To do what is right and just is more acceptable to the Lord
than sacrifice.

Proverbs 21.3 (Judaeo-Christian)

88 Let a man put away anger, forsake pride,
and overcome all bondage.

Dhammapada 221 (Buddhism)

89 When you are in public life,
any lapse in conduct can bring disfavor.

I Ching 16.1 (Taoism)

90 Show proper respect to everyone.

1 Peter 2.17 (Christianity)

91 At all times and in all you do
Provide for yourself with care.

Mila Grubum (Buddhism)

92 The simple heart finds no hard way,
good thought finds no wounds.

The Odes of Solomon 34 (Christianity)

93 If the mind does not feel complacency in the conduct, the
nature becomes starved.

Mencius 2 (Confucianism)

94 Don't draw another's bow,
Don't ride another's horse,
Don't discuss another's faults,
Don't explore another's affairs.

Mumonkan 45 (Zen)

95 Give careful thought to your ways.

Haggai 1.5 (Judaeo-Christian)

96 Where a gentleman is ignorant, one would expect him not to
offer any opinion.

Analects XIII.3 (Confucianism)

97 Be neither miserly nor prodigal, for then you should either be
    reproached or be reduced to penury.
                Koran 17.21 (Islam)

98 Even a child is known by his actions,
      by whether his conduct is pure and right.
                Proverbs 20.11 (Judaeo-Christian)

99 A wise man lets neither men nor words go to waste.
                Analects XV.8 (Confucianism)

100 The greatest concerns of men are these,
       to make who is an enemy a friend,
       to make him who is wicked righteous,
       and to make him who is ignorant learned.
                Shayast-na-shayast XX.6 (Zoroastrianism)

101 What is right to do, do it willingly.
                The Sentences
                of Sextus XII.34.6–7 (Gnosticism)

102 Real words are not vain,
       Vain words are not real;
     And since those who argue prove nothing
       A sensible man does not argue.
                Tao Teh Ching 81 (Taoism)

103 Never remain silent when a word might put things right.
                Ecclesiasticus 4.23 (Judaeo-Christian)

104 One does not explain away what is already done,
       one does not argue against what is already accomplished,
       and one does not condemn what has already gone by.
                Analects III.21 (Confucianism)

105 The sword of a virtuous character and upright conduct is
     sharper than blades of steel.
                Epistle to the Son of the Wolf 29 (Baha'i)

106   Teach the older man to be temperate, worthy of respect, self-controlled, and sound in faith, in love, and in endurance.
    Titus 2.2 (Christianity)

107   No matter by whom or where or how provoked,
        never do you transgress your own fair path of conduct.
    Satapancasatkastotra XI.118 (Buddhism)

108   A man must insult himself before others will.
    Mencius 4.1.8 (Confucianism)

109   A fool finds pleasure in evil conduct,
        but a man of understanding delights in wisdom.
    Proverbs 10.23 (Judaeo-Christian)

110   If life is a gamble then gamble away all your lust and your anger, your envy and pride.
    Adi Granth (Sikhism)

111   At no time in the world will a man who is sane
    Over-reach himself,
    Over-spend himself,
    Over-rate himself.
    Tao Teh Ching 29 (Taoism)

112   A man's ways are in full view of the Lord,
        and he examines all his paths.
    Proverbs 5.21 (Judaeo-Christian)

113   Being fond of courage while detesting poverty will lead men to unruly behaviour.
    Analects VIII.10 (Confucianism)

DEATH

114   All that has a beginning must have an end.
    Mahavagga 6.35.6 (Buddhism)

115   We are born as from a quiet sleep,
        and we die to a calm awakening.
                    Chuang-tzu VI (Taoism)

116   For all things born in truth must die,
        and out of death in truth comes life.
                    Bhagavad Gita 2.27 (Hinduism)

117   Do not be smug over another man's death;
        remember that we must all die.
                    Ecclesiasticus 8.7 (Judaeo-Christian)

118   Birth and death are both illusions.
                    Mila Grubum (Buddhism)

119   To be born is to come out; to die is to return.
                    Tao Teh Ching 50 (Taoism)

120   In pride is man born, in pride he dieth.
                    Asa Ki War 7 (Sikhism)

121   By one man sin entered the world, and death by sin;
        and so death passed upon all men.
                    Romans 5.12 (Christianity)

122   Birth is not a beginning: death is not an end.
                    Chuang-tzu (Taoism)

123   Sleep is brother to death.
                    Hadith 111 (Islam)

124   If death come at night, may healing come at dawn.
                    Avesta (Zoroastrianism)

125   Envy, passion, and hatred drive a man toward death.
                    The Sayings of the Fathers 2.16 (Judaism)

126   Weep for the living rather than for the dead.
                    Jatakas 317 (Buddhism)

127   The Spirit that is in all beings is immortal in them all: for the
       death of what cannot die, ceases thou to sorrow.
                        Bhagavad Gita 2.30 (Hinduism)

128   All go to the same place;
           all come from dust, and to dust all return.
                        Ecclesiastes 3.20 (Judaeo-Christian)

129   If repeatedly and continuously one thinks about death, he
       can easily conquer the demon of laziness.
                        Mila Grubum (Buddhism)

130   The fear of [death] grieves man because of the ignorance of
       the soul.
                        The Sentences of Sextus XII.28.10–12
                        (Gnosticism)

131   All men in this world must inescapably come to their end,
       and if a thing is inevitable, what point is there grieving over
       it?
                        Mahabharata (Hinduism)

132   Even in death the righteous have a refuge.
                        Proverbs 14.32 (Judaeo-Christian)

133   All is mortal save the face of God.
                        Gleanings from the
                        Writings of Baha'u'llah (Baha'i)

134   The wise grieve not for those who live;
           and they grieve not for those who die
           —for life and death shall pass away.
                        Bhagavad Gita 2.11 (Hinduism)

135   Call no man happy before he dies,
           for not until death is a man known for what he is.
                        Ecclesiasticus 11.28 (Judaeo-Christian)

136 One who identifies himself with his soul regards bodily transmigration of his soul at death fearlessly, like changing one cloth for another.
Samadhi Shataka (Jainism)

137 You may recognize death but do not understand it.
Tibetan Book of the Dead (Buddhism)

138 Death is swallowed up in victory.
1 Corinthians 15.54 (Christianity)

139 Know that death is unreal, and everything else that appeareth is unreal.
Adi Granth (Sikhism)

140 Know that life is unreal and death is also unreal.
Tibetan Book of the Dead (Buddhism)

141 By your own attitudes you can bring yourself life or you can bring yourself death.
Gorikai (Shinto)

142 If you do not think of the end, it will be full of distress, even of the greatest.
Shu King 5.17.2 (Confucianism)

143 If you aren't afraid of dying,
there is nothing you can't achieve.
Tao Teh Ching 74 (Taoism)

144 Life is but a loan to man; death is the creditor who will one day claim it.
Talmud (Judaism)

145 Know that you will experience sights and sounds after death regardless of your religion and the extent to which you practiced it.
Tibetan Book of the Dead (Buddhism)

146   Look on death as going home.
Chuang-tzu XVII.9 (Taoism)

DECISION
---

147   Let us discern for ourselves what is right.
Job 34.4 (Judaeo-Christian)

148   Men must be decided on what they will NOT do,
and then they are able to act with vigour in what they
ought to do.
Mencius 4 (Confucianism)

149   If you have the slightest choice of right and wrong,
you will fall into confusion of mind.
Hekiganroku 51 (Zen)

150   Consult not with a fool, for he cannot keep counsel.
Ecclesiasticus 8.17 (Judaeo-Christian)

151   You cannot have things both ways: making a choice means
abandoning its alternative.
I Ching 17.2 (Taoism)

152   Choose for yourself righteousness, and a good life.
The Book of Enoch 93.4 (Judaism)

153   Just decisions should be thy prayers.
Adi Granth (Sikhism)

154   The perfect Way is only difficult for those who pick and
choose.
On Trust in the Heart (Zen)

155 Discretion will protect you,
and understanding will guard you.
Proverbs 2.11 (Judaeo-Christian)

156 Exercise choice at one's own free will.
Yasna 31.11 (Zoroastrianism)

157 When right and wrong are intermingled,
even the holy ones cannot distinguish between them.
Hekiganroku 41 (Zen)

158 Make plans by seeking advice.
Proverbs 20.18 (Judaeo-Christian)

159 How can one lay down a rule by which to distinguish right
from wrong?
Nihongi XXII (Shinto)

160 A double-minded man is unstable in all his ways.
James 1.8 (Christianity)

161 He who weighs matters in the balance,
And makes his choice accordingly —
He is the real wise one.
Dhammapada 268 (Buddhism)

162 Those who argue about right and wrong are those enslaved
by right and wrong.
Mumonkan 18 (Zen)

163 The lot is cast into the lap,
but its every decision is from the Lord.
Proverbs 16.33 (Judaeo-Christian)

164 Decisions on important matters should not be made by one
person alone.
Nihongi XXII (Shinto)

DEEDS

165 He that does a good deed shall be repaid tenfold;
but he that does evil shall be rewarded with evil.
Koran 6.160 (Islam)

166 There is a way of escape from every other enemy:
but ill deeds never die but pursue and destroy their author.
Tirukkural (Hinduism)

167 God will render to every man according to his deeds.
Romans 2.6 (Christianity)

168 An evil deed, like freshly drawn milk,
does not turn sour at once.
Dhammapada 71 (Buddhism)

169 No deed arising from a renouncing heart is small,
and no deed arising from an avaricious heart is fruitful.
The Book of Wisdom 45 (Sufism)

170 For if you do what is true,
your ways will prosper through your deeds.
Tobit 4.6 (Judaeo-Christian)

171 A man does evil deeds by going on the wrong path through
desire, through hatred, through delusion, and through
fear.
Digha-Nikaya III.181 (Buddhism)

172 You are alone, you have no companion:
you will suffer the consequences of your deeds.
Songs of Kabir LXXV (Sikhism)

173 The wise man does not teach by words but by deeds.
Tao Teh Ching 2 (Taoism)

174 Do the right, the right, the right,
  Till the breath of death;
  Shun the wrong, although the right
  Leads to death of breath.
        Panchatantra I (Hinduism)

175 The rule is that one is to proceed with great delibera-
  tion when he knoweth not if it be a sin or a good deed; in
  such cases, it is not to be done.
        Shayast-na-shayast X.25 (Zoroastrianism)

176 Greater is he who causes good deeds than he who does them.
        Talmud (Judaism)

177 Evil men know not what should be done or what should not
  be done.
        Bhagavad Gita 16.7 (Hinduism)

178 What it is [not right to do],
  do not even consider [doing it].
        The Sentences of Sextus XII.16.24–25
        (Gnosticism)

179 Virtuous deeds are set going by him who teaches learned
  sayings.
        Dinkard 9.63.10 (Zoroastrianism)

180 To God I commit my cause.
        Manual of Discipline (Judaism)

181 Even a flight in the air cannot free you from suffering after the
  deed which is evil has once been committed.
        Dharmapada (Buddhism)

182 It is through your deeds that ye can distinguish yourself from
  others.
        Gleanings from the
        Writings of Baha'u'llah (Baha'i)

183   Do nothing out of selfish ambition or vain conceit.
Philippians 2.3 (Christianity)

184   Benefit to oneself and to others can never be achieved through
sloth; Strive, therefore, to do good deeds.
Mila Grubum (Buddhism)

185   True compassion is known by its good deeds.
Tao Teh Ching 38 (Taoism)

186   Claims made immodestly are difficult to live up to.
Analects XIV.20 (Confucianism)

187   Keep your promises;
you are accountable for all that you promise.
Koran 17.34 (Islam)

188   The gentleman is ashamed of his word outstripping his deed.
Analects XIV.27 (Confucianism)

189   The deed proves the promise.
Hitopadesa (Hinduism)

DELUSION

190   Do not deceive yourselves.
1 Corinthians 3.18 (Christianity)

191   From delusion lead me to Truth.
From darkness lead me to Light.
From death lead me to immortality.
Brihad-Aranyaka
Upanishad I.3.28 (Hinduism)

192 Misery is gone in the case of a man who has no delusion.
Nirgrantha-Pravachana 2.28 (Jainism)

193 Woe to those who are wise in their own eyes and clever in their own sight.
Isaiah 5.21 (Judaeo-Christian)

194 For what greater fool can there be than the man who has obtained this rare human birth together with bodily and mental strength and yet fails, through delusion, to realize his own highest good?
Viveka Chidamani (Hinduism)

195 Presuming to know is a disease.
Tao Teh Ching 71 (Taoism)

196 Many false prophets will appear and deceive many.
Matthew 24.11 (Christianity)

197 Cast aside your own delusions; then you will be no different from the sages of the past.
Tan Ching 12 (Zen)

198 For the (enjoyment) of this world is a (lie),
and its gold and its silver is error.
The Dialogue
of the Saviour III.141.17–19 (Gnosticism)

199 When thy mind leaves behind its dark forest of delusion, thou shalt go beyond the scriptures of times past and still to come.
Bhagavad Gita 2.52 (Hinduism)

200 The thief who finds no opportunity to steal thinks himself an honest man.
Talmud (Judaism)

201 Every one is perfect to himself:
no man admitteth himself wanting.
Asa Ki War (Sikhism)

202 Do not merely listen to the word,
and so deceive yourselves. Do what it says.
James 1.22 (Christianity)

203 Like a mirage in summer,
so palpitates the deluded mind.
Lankavatara Sutra (Buddhism)

204 Those who dream of the banquet,
wake to lamentation and sorrow.
Chuang-tzu (Taoism)

205 The man who thinks he knows something does not yet know
as he ought to know.
1 Corinthians 8.2 (Christianity)

206 It would be mere delusion, however, to call yourself omni-
scient, when you know nothing.
Lotus Sutra V.71 (Buddhism)

207 Delusion is gone in the case of him who has no desire.
Nirgrantha-Pravachana 2.28 (Jainism)

208 Man sees the mote in his neighbor's eye,
but knows not of the beam in his own.
Talmud (Judaism)

209 All beings are born in delusion, the delusion of division
which comes from desire and hate.
Bhagavad Gita 7.27 (Hinduism)

DESIRE

210 A longing fulfilled is sweet to the soul,
  but fools detest turning from evil.
                    Proverbs 13.19 (Judaeo-Christian)

211 As thou dost desire, so shalt thou be.
                    Yasna 71.16 (Zoroastrianism)

212 All is clouded by desire: as fire by smoke, as a mirror by dust,
  as an unborn babe by its covering.
                    Bhagavad Gita 3.38 (Hinduism)

213 Where there is no desire, all things are at peace.
                    Tao Teh Ching 37 (Taoism)

214 Ye desire the passing fruitions of this world,
  but God desireth the next life for you.
                    Koran 8 (Islam)

215 When a man surrenders all desires that come to the heart and
  by the grace of God finds the joy of God, then his soul has
  indeed found peace.
                    Bhagavad Gita 2.55 (Hinduism)

216 If you yourself were not a man of desires,
  no one would steal even if stealing carried a reward.
                    Analects XII.18 (Confucianism)

217 Strong desire is the origin of pain.
                    Lotus Sutra (Buddhism)

218 God cannot be seen so long as there is the slightest taint of
  desire; therefore have thy small desires satisfied, and re-
  nounce the big desires by right reasoning and discrimina-
  tion.
                    The Sayings of Sri Ramakrishna (Hinduism)

219   Abstain from sinful desires,
          which war against your soul.
                          1 Peter 2.11 (Christianity)

220   There is no net like illusion,
          and no rushing torrent like desire.
                          Dhammapada 251 (Buddhism)

221   A man should not excite his desires by medicines nor satisfy
          them with unnatural objects or in public or holy places.
                          Laws of Manu (Hinduism)

222   The more you get, the more you want;
          your desires increase with your means.
                          Uttara-Dhyayana Sutra 8.17 (Jainism)

223   After desire has conceived, it gives birth to sin;
          and sin, when it is full-grown, gives birth to death.
                          James 1.15 (Christianity)

224   Do your earthly duty free from desire,
          and you shall well perform your heavenly purpose.
                          Bhagavad Gita 3 (Hinduism)

225   Desire not the world, and God will love you;
          and desire not what other men have,
          and they will love you.
                          Hadith 182 (Islam)

226   Pain is medicine, worldly pleasure a disease;
          where there is such pleasure,
          there is no desire for God.
                          Adi Granth (Sikhism)

227   For mind-development there is nothing better than restrict-
          ing one's desires.
                          Mencius 7.2.35 (Confucianism)

228 Concern yourselves with the things that benefit mankind,
and not with your corrupt and selfish desires.
Epistle to the Son of the Wolf 29 (Baha'i)

229 When all desires that cling to the heart disappear,
then a mortal becomes immortal, and even
in this life attains Liberation.
The Supreme Teaching (Hinduism)

DESTINY

230 It is according to destiny that one speaks, eats, hears, sees,
and takes breath.
Adi Granth (Sikhism)

231 You do not know what will happen tomorrow.
James 4.14 (Christianity)

232 What shall not be, will never be;
What shall be, follows painlessly;
The thing that your fingers grasp, will flit,
If fate has predetermined it.
Panchatantra I (Hinduism)

233 Whatever mishap befalls you, it is on account of something
which you have done.
Hadith 300 (Islam)

234 The great man must crumble;
the strong beam must break;
and the wise man wither away like a plant.
Li Ki 2.1.2 (Confucianism)

235 Do not worry about tomorrow,
for tomorrow will worry about itself.
Matthew 6.34 (Christianity)

236 A man gets in life what he is fated to get.
                Garuda Purana (Hinduism)

237 When we realize that all things are the activity of Heaven,
          then we know neither pain nor care.
                Kojiki (Shinto)

238 It is possible for everything to change but divine providence.
                Shayast-na-shayast XX.17 (Zoroastrianism)

239 Those who sow in summer reap in winter.
                Gospel of Phillip II.52.25 (Gnosticism)

240 Fate links the unlinked, unlinks links;
          It links the things that no man thinks.
                Panchatantra II (Hinduism)

241 In his heart a man plans his course,
          but the Lord determines his steps.
                Proverbs 16.9 (Judaeo-Christian)

242 What is written from the beginning,
          no one will blot out.
                Adi Granth (Sikhism)

243 Recognize, accept, be one with whatever happens to you.
                Tibetan Book of the Dead 15 (Buddhism)

244 That which God writes on thy forehead,
          thou wilt come to it.
                Koran (Islam)

245 The written destiny no one effaces.
                Adi Granth (Sikhism)

246 Whether the world is eternal or not, whether it is limited or
          infinite, what is certain is that birth, old age, death, and
          suffering exist.
                Samyutta Nikaya (Buddhism)

247 A man reaps what he sows.
                    Galatians 6.7 (Christianity)

248 Good luck or ill luck, if man will find it,
      It is fate that found it, not his own doing.
                    Mahabharata (Hinduism)

249 Not a breath do you expire but a Decree of Destiny makes it
      go forth.
                    The Book of Wisdom 22 (Sufism)

250 All share a common destiny – the righteous and the wicked,
      the good and the bad, the clean and the unclean, those
      who offer sacrifices and those who do not.
                    Ecclesiastes 9.2 (Judaeo-Christian)

251 A man is the creator of his own fate,
      and even in his fetal life he is affected
      by the dynamics of his prior existence.
                    Garuda Purana (Hinduism)

252 Destiny is a helper in virtue.
                    Menog-i Khrad 3.7 (Zoroastrianism)

253 Creatures follow the destiny of their deeds.
                    Iti-vuttaka 99 (Buddhism)

254 Destiny is master today – Man was master yesterday.
                    Hitopadesa (Hinduism)

255 A mortal's way is [not] of himself,
      neither can a man direct his own steps.
                    Manual of Discipline (Judaism)

256 Men cannot forestall their doom,
      nor can they retard it.
                    Koran 15.5 (Islam)

257 A man's steps are directed by the Lord.
                    Proverbs 20.24 (Judaeo-Christian)

DISCIPLINE

258 In the way in which a man wishes to walk he is guided.
Talmud (Judaism)

259 A fine horse runs even at the shadow of the whip.
Hekiganroku 65 (Zen)

260 Blessed is the man whom God corrects;
so do not despise the discipline of the Almighty.
Job 5.17 (Judaeo-Christian)

261 Without a certain amount of discipline,
you will not get what you seek.
I Ching 32.4 (Taoism)

262 The Lord disciplines those he loves.
Hebrews 12.6 (Christianity)

263 He who is illumined at the beginning is illumined at the end.
The Book of Wisdom 27 (Sufism)

264 If you realize the first, you master the last.
Mumonkan 13 (Zen)

265 Whoever loves discipline loves knowledge,
but he who hates correction is stupid.
Proverbs 12.1 (Judaeo-Christian)

266 He who knoweth the precepts by heart,
but faileth to practise them,
Is like unto one who lighteth a lamp
and then shutteth his eyes.
The Ocean of Delight for the Wise (Buddhism)

267 Do not follow what you do not know.
Koran 17.36 (Islam)

268   Let us receive correction,
          at which no man ought to repine.
                    The First Epistle of Clement
                    to the Corinthians 23.3 (Christianity)

269   If one sets strict standards for oneself and makes allowances
        for others when making demands on them, one will stay
        clear of ill will.
                    Analects XV.15 (Confucianism)

270   Though hundreds the gate may enter,
          Few can keep the disciplines.
                    Mila Grubum (Buddhism)

271   He who heeds discipline shows the way to life,
          but whoever ignores correction leads others astray.
                    Proverbs 10.17 (Judaeo-Christian)

272   He who merely knows right principles is not equal to him
        who loves them.
                    Analects (Confucianism)

273   He who is a slave against his will will be able to become free.
                    Gospel of Phillip II.79.13–14 (Gnosticism)

274   Be eager for discipline,
          that you may acquire righteousness.
                    Uttara-Dhyayana Sutra I.7 (Jainism)

275   A man can only do things when he knows what things he will
        not do.
                    Mencius 4.2.8 (Confucianism)

276   Strength without discipline will lead not to victory, but
        defeat.
                    I Ching 7.1 (Taoism)

277   Endure hardship as discipline;
          God is treating you as sons.
                    Hebrews 12.7 (Christianity)

278   Attend strictly to the commands of your parents and the
      instructions of your teachers.
                        An Oracle of the Deity Temmangu (Shinto)

279   Make a fence to thy words.
                        Talmud (Judaism)

280   Train a child in the way he should go,
          and when he is old he will not turn from it.
                        Proverbs 22.6 (Judaeo-Christian)

EDUCATION

281   The best instruction is not in words.
                        Tao Teh Ching 43 (Taoism)

282   Teach me, and I will be quiet;
          show me where I have been wrong.
                        Job 6.24 (Judaeo-Christian)

283   Be devoted to your master's teachings,
          and the Innate will become manifest.
                        Saraha's Treasury of Songs 57 (Buddhism)

284   It is only the most intelligent and the most stupid who are not
      susceptible to change.
                        Analects XVII.3 (Confucianism)

285   The true teacher, having taught me love,
          Hath caused me to meet God.
                        Hymns of Guru Nanak (Sikhism)

286   Return to the Root and you will find the meaning.
                        On Trust in the Heart (Zen)

287 Do not neglect the studies of the learned,
     but apply yourself to their maxims.
                    Ecclesiasticus 8.8 (Judaeo-Christian)

288 When you are studying the scriptures,
     Let there be no intellectual conceits.
                    Mila Grubum (Buddhism)

289 The object of learning is nothing else but to seek for the lost
     mind.
                    Mencius (Confucianism)

290 How shall teaching help him who is without understanding?
                    Hitopadesa 3.117 (Hinduism)

291 Be ready to listen to every narrative,
     and do not let wise proverbs escape you.
                    Ecclesiasticus 6.35 (Judaeo-Christian)

292 To be fond of learning is to be near to knowledge.
                    Doctrine of the Mean (Confucianism)

293 The beginning of all learning is the knowledge of religion.
                    Talmud (Judaism)

294 Rewards and punishments are the lowest form of education.
                    Chuang-tzu (Taoism)

295 To learn and never be filled is wisdom;
     to teach and never be weary is love.
                    Mencius 2.1.2 (Confucianism)

296 The shy cannot learn; the irascible cannot teach.
                    The Sayings of the Fathers 2.6 (Judaism)

297 Teaching is the half of learning.
                    Shu King 4.8 (Confucianism)

298 Learn by teaching.
> Talmud (Judaism)

299 A man is worthy of being a teacher who gets to know what is new by keeping fresh in his mind what he is already familiar with.
> Analects II.11 (Confucianism)

300 It is good to teach;
if what he says he does likewise.
> Epistle of Ignatius
> to the Ephesians 3.19 (Christianity)

301 If he cannot make himself correct,
what business has he with making others correct?
> Analects XIII.13 (Confucianism)

302 The best teacher is time.
> Talmud (Judaism)

303 So he who knows, he who is well-composed,
Full of deep learning and unshakeable,
He surely will make others understand
Who sit beside and listen heedfully.
> Samyutta-Nikaya X.321 (Buddhism)

304 The bad man is the lesson of the good.
> Tao Teh Ching 27 (Taoism)

305 You must teach what is in accord with sound doctrine.
> Titus 2.1 (Christianity)

306 If you set an example by being correct,
who would dare to remain incorrect?
> Analects XII.17 (Confucianism)

307 One's own true nature cannot be explained by another,
But it is revealed by one's master's instruction.
> Saraha's Treasury of Songs 38 (Buddhism)

308 The mind is the guide, but reason is the teacher.
       The Teachings
       of Silvanus VII.85.25–26 (Gnosticism)

309 He considers those who point out his faults as his most
       benevolent teachers.
       Tao Teh Ching 61 (Taoism)

310 Let him find first what is right and then he can teach it to
       others, avoiding thus useless pain.
       Dhammapada 158 (Buddhism)

311 Instruct a wise man and he will be wiser still;
       teach a righteous man and he will add to his learning.
       Proverbs 9.11 (Judaeo-Christian)

312 Can you do your best for anyone without educating him?
       Analects XIV.7 (Confucianism)

313 Be cautious when you teach; for an error in teaching may
       amount to the presumption of sin.
       The Sayings of the Fathers 4.16 (Judaism)

314 A man who goes over what he has already learned and gains
       some new understanding from it is worthy to be a teacher.
       Analects X (Confucianism)

315 You, then, who teach others,
       do you not teach yourself?
       Romans 2.21 (Christianity)

ENVY

316 Do not envy a violent man, or choose any of his ways.
       Proverbs 3.31 (Judaeo-Christian)

317 With the aid of craving does one eliminate craving.
    Anguttara Nikaya (Buddhism)

318 Do not be envious of each other.
    Forty-Two Traditions of An-Nawawi (Islam)

319 Where you have envy and selfish ambition,
    there you will find disorder and every evil practice.
    James 3.16 (Christianity)

320 If we envy others, they in turn will envy us:
    the evil of envy knows no limit.
    Nihongi XXII (Shinto)

321 The chase of gain is rich in hate.
    Analects IV.12 (Confucianism)

322 Resentment kills a fool, and envy slays the simple.
    Job 5.2 (Judaeo-Christian)

323 Covetousness is a dog.
    Adi Granth (Sikhism)

324 Envy not the glory of a sinner:
    for you know not what shall be his end.
    Ecclesiasticus 9.11 (Judaeo-Christian)

325 No blessing is so great as a nature that is free from all envy.
    Tirukkural (Hinduism)

326 A heart at peace gives life to the body,
    but envy rots the bones.
    Proverbs 14.30 (Judaeo-Christian)

327 Don't envy beauty.
    T'ai Shang Kan Ying P'ien (Taoism)

328 Envy, cupidity, and ambition lead a man to death.
    The Sayings of the Fathers 4.28 (Judaism)

329 Covet no wealth of any man.
                    Yajurveda XL.1 (Hinduism)

330 If you harbor bitter envy and selfish ambition in your hearts,
     do not boast about it or deny the truth.
                    James 3.14 (Christianity)

331 The monk who feels envy cannot achieve deep contempla-
     tion.
                    Dhammapada 365 (Buddhism)

332 The envious man has a wicked eye.
                    Ecclesiasticus 14.8 (Judaeo-Christian)

ERROR

333 Not to mend one's ways when one has erred is to err indeed.
                    Analects XV.30 (Confucianism)

334 Avoid the little faults as well as the great.
                    Ecclesiastes 5.15 (Judaeo-Christian)

335 Don't rank faults as crimes.
                    T'ai Shang Kan Ying P'ien (Taoism)

336 The real fault is to have faults and not try to amend them.
                    Analects XV.29 (Confucianism)

337 Another's faults are plainly seen;
     it is hard to see one's own.
                    Jatakas 374 (Buddhism)

338 Indeed, Allah does not in any way wrong mankind,
     but they wrong themselves.
                    Koran 10.40 (Islam)

339 Do not be ashamed of mistakes,
and go on to make them crimes.
Shu King 4.8.2 (Confucianism)

340 I have acted like a fool and erred greatly.
1 Samuel 26.21 (Judaeo-Christian)

341 Conceal not the good qualities of others;
and fail not to correct that which is wrong when you see it.
Nihongi XXII (Shinto)

342 The wrong in others is not your own crime,
your own wrong is of itself your crime.
Tan Ching 36 (Zen)

343 The vile are ever prone to detect the faults of others, though
they may be as small as mustard seeds, and persistently
shut their eyes against their own, though they be as large
as Vilva fruits.
Garuda Purana (Hinduism)

344 Stay away from wrong, and it will turn away from you.
Ecclesiasticus 7.2 (Judaeo-Christian)

345 Things never err, they always follow their principle.
Chou-ilueh-li (Taoism)

346 Clearly, we see others' faults
But seldom do we see our own.
Mila Grubum (Buddhism)

347 A gentleman blames himself,
while a common man blames others.
Analects V (Confucianism)

348 If you blame someone else,
there is no end to the blame.
Tao Teh Ching 79 (Taoism)

349 To blame others is no good.
         Sutra-krit-anga I.2.2.2 (Jainism)

350 He that seeks guidance shall be guided to his own advantage,
       but he that errs shall err at his own peril.
         Koran 17.8 (Islam)

351 When you make a mistake do not be afraid of mending your
       ways.
         Analects IX.25 (Confucianism)

352 When the grace of God descends on him, each one will
       understand his own mistakes.
         The Sayings of Sri Ramakrishna (Hinduism)

353 You are in error because you do not know the Scriptures or
       the power of God.
         Matthew 22.29 (Christianity)

354 When an inferior man does a wrong thing,
       he is sure to gloss it over.
         Analects XIX.8 (Confucianism)

355 I have taught that when error ceases,
       You should know yourself for what you are.
         Saraha's Treasury of Songs 60 (Buddhism)

356 Confess your faults one to another,
       and pray one for another, that ye may be healed.
         James 5.16 (Christianity)

357 The gentleman's errors are like an eclipse of the sun and
       moon in that when he errs the whole world sees him doing
       so and when he reforms the whole world looks up to him.
         Analects XIX.21 (Confucianism)

358 One shows the faults of others like chaff winnowed in the
       wind, but one conceals one's own faults as a cunning
       gambler conceals his dice.
         Dhammapada 252 (Buddhism)

359 If you do not do what is right,
   sin is crouching at your door.
                    Genesis 4.7 (Judaeo-Christian)

360 A man who knows his error is not greatly in error.
                    Chuang-tzu XII (Taoism)

361 Observe the errors and you will know the man.
                    Analects IV.7 (Confucianism)

EVIL

362 Whoever has done an atom's weight of good shall see it, and
   whoever has done an atom's weight of evil shall see it also.
                    Koran 99.8 (Islam)

363 To shun evil is understanding.
                    Job 28.28 (Judaeo-Christian)

364 The evil of men is that they like to be the teachers of others.
                    Mencius 4.1.23 (Confucianism)

365 A man may find pleasure in evil as long as his evil has not
   given fruit; but when the fruit of evil comes, then that man
   finds good indeed.
                    Dhammapada 119 (Buddhism)

366 Those who plow evil and sow trouble reap it.
                    Job 4.8 (Judaeo-Christian)

367 By doing evil the self becomes a rogue,
   an animal or inhabitant of hell.
                    Pravacana-sara 1.12 (Jainism)

368 It is better to sit alone than in the company of evil.
Hadith 170 (Islam)

369 Man quits not his evil habits.
Adi Granth (Sikhism)

370 The love of money is a root of all kinds of evil.
1 Timothy 6.10 (Christianity)

371 The love of the world is the root of all evil.
Hadith 433 (Islam)

372 Neither in the sky, or deep in the ocean,
nor in a mountain cave, nor anywhere,
can a man be free from the evil he has done.
Dhammapada 127 (Buddhism)

373 Do no evil, and evil will never befall you.
Ecclesiasticus 7.1 (Judaeo-Christian)

374 He is evil who is the best to the evil.
Yasna 46.6 (Zoroastrianism)

375 If you see the evil others do,
and if you feel you disapprove,
Be careful not to do likewise,
for people's deeds remain with them.
Dharmapada (Buddhism)

376 They that have done good shall have everlasting life;
and they that have done evil shall have everlasting damnation.
Helaman 12.26 (Mormonism)

377 Give evil nothing to oppose and it will disappear by itself.
Tao Teh Ching 60 (Taoism)

378 Deceitfulness, insolence and self-conceit,
    anger and harshness and ignorance
    —these belong to a man who is born for hell.
                 Bhagavad Gita 16.4 (Hinduism)

379 He who denies guilt doubles his guilt.
                 Talmud (Judaism)

380 There is no fire like lust,
    and no chains like those of hate.
                 Dhammapada 251 (Buddhism)

381 Wrong not and you will not be wronged.
                 Koran 2.279 (Islam)

382 Few men are utterly bad.
                 Nihongi XXII (Shinto)

383 The wicked are destined to see the Deviser of Evil as thin as a
    thread of hair.
                 Zohar (Kabbalah)

384 Even as rust on iron destroys in the end the iron,
    a man's own impure transgressions lead that man
    to the evil path.
                 Dhammapada 240 (Buddhism)

FAITH

385 Faith is being sure of what we hope for and certain of what
    we do not see.
                 Hebrews 11.1 (Christianity)

386 Belief in things ascertained as they are is right belief.
                 Tattvartha Sutra 1.2 (Jainism)

387 A people without faith cannot stand.
            Analects XII.7 (Confucianism)

388 Blessed are they that have not seen,
         and yet have believed.
            John 20.29 (Christianity)

389 Man is made of faith: as his faith is so he is.
            Bhagavad Gita 17.3 (Hinduism)

390 Use no means but a pure faith.
            Adi Granth (Sikhism)

391 Faith without works is dead.
            James 2.20 (Christianity)

392 Modesty and charity are parts of faith.
            Hadith 55 (Islam)

393 Faith and resignation are the characteristics of the holy.
            Hymns of Guru Nanak (Sikhism)

394 We live by faith, not by sight.
            2 Corinthians 5.7 (Christianity)

395 With the heart one knows faith.
            Brihad-Aranyaka
            Upanishad 3.9.21 (Hinduism)

396 Faith, if insufficient,
         is apt to become no faith at all.
            Tao Teh Ching 17 (Taoism)

397 If a man has faith and has virtue,
         then he has true glory and treasure.
            Dhammapada 303 (Buddhism)

398 Faith can achieve miracles,
       while vanity or egoism is the death of man.
                    The Sayings of Sri Ramakrishna (Hinduism)

399 That he may know that thy faithfulness is stronger than the
       cords of death.
                    Doctrine and Covenants (Mormonism)

400 Little faith is put in those who have little faith.
                    Tao Teh Ching 23 (Taoism)

401 The only thing that counts is faith expressing itself through
       love.
                    Galatians 5.6 (Christianity)

402 Good faith is the foundation of right.
                    Nihongi XXII (Shinto)

403 Patience is half the faith.
                    Talmud (Judaism)

404 The faith of no man can be conditioned by anyone but
       himself.
                    Gleanings from the
                    Writings of Bah'u'llah 143 (Baha'i)

405 Put all your trust in the Lord and do not rely on your own
       understanding.
                    Proverbs 3.5 (Judaeo-Christian)

406 Blessed are those who have faith and do good works; blissful
       their end.
                    Koran 13.25 (Islam)

407 Man in truth is made of faith.
                    Chandogya Upanishad 3.14 (Hinduism)

408 Faith is like a tree, and reliance like a fruit.
                    The Book of Faith and Reliance (Kabbalah)

409 Faith is the best wealth to a man here.
> Sutta Nipata 181 (Buddhism)

410 Kindness is the mark of faith;
> whoever has no kindness can have no faith.
> Hadith 254 (Islam)

411 The righteous shall live by faith.
> Romans 1.17 (Christianity)

412 He that denies the faith shall gain nothing from his labours.
> Koran 5.5 (Islam)

413 The faithful do not speak many words,
> but their works are numerous.
> The Sentences of Sextus XII.33.24–25
> (Gnosticism)

414 By faith comes knowledge of the truth.
> Yajurveda XIX.30 (Hinduism)

415 The believer should have a faith which makes him a friend of God.
> Gorikai (Shinto)

416 The righteous man will live by being faithful.
> Habakkuk 2.4 (Judaeo-Christian)

417 By faith you shall be free and go beyond the realm of death.
> Sutta Nipata 1146 (Buddhism)

418 Avoid those that treat their faith as a sport and a pastime and are seduced by the life of this world.
> Koran 6.70 (Islam)

419 As his faith is in this life,
> so he becomes in the beyond.
> Chandogya Upanishad 3.14 (Hinduism)

FALSEHOOD

420 The punishment of the liar is that he is not believed.
> Talmud (Judaism)

421 Do not lie about yourself.
> Tibetan Book of the Dead (Buddhism)

422 Better to be poor than a liar.
> Proverbs 19.22 (Judaeo-Christian)

423 Those who speak falsely from pride of knowledge are not
capable of many virtues.
> Sutra-krit-anga I.13.3 (Jainism)

424 You have not lied to men but to God.
> Acts 5.4 (Christianity)

425 Abandon falsehood; pursue truth.
> Adi Granth (Sikhism)

426 What force would never try may be achieved by fraud.
> Hitopadesa (Hinduism)

427 Falsehood is common, truth is rare.
> Talmud (Judaism)

428 For he is himself a liar who is very good to a liar,
he is a righteous man to whom a righteous man is dear.
> Yasna 46.6 (Zoroastrianism)

429 A thief is better to a man who is accustomed to a lie.
> Ecclesiasticus 20.25 (Judaeo-Christian)

430 Confound not truth with falsehood;
nor knowingly hide the truth.
> Koran 2.43 (Islam)

431   Even when his Scripture learning is astonishing, the cheat
remains a cheat.

Hitopadesa (Hinduism)

432   A lie has no feet.

Talmud (Judaism)

433   O good man if thou shouldest speak falsely,
all thy pure deeds would go for naught.

Laws of Manu 8.90 (Hinduism)

434   Do not help a wicked man by being a malicious witness.

Exodus 23.1 (Judaeo-Christian)

435   It is by not believing people that you turn them into liars.

Tao Teh Ching 17 (Taoism)

436   The Lord abhors dishonest scales,
but accurate weights are his delight.

Proverbs 11.1 (Judaeo-Christian)

437   There is no higher virtue than veracity nor heavier crime
than falsehood.

Narada Smriti 1.226 (Hinduism)

438   Let none of you attend to the liar's words and commands; he
leads house, clan, district and country into misery and
destruction.

Yasna 31.18 (Zoroastrianism)

439   From that thing which is false what truth can come?

Ecclesiasticus 34.4 (Judaeo-Christian)

FAMILY

440 Regard heaven as your father, earth as your mother,
and all things as your brothers and sisters.
Oracle of the Deity Atsuta (Shinto)

441 Remember that through your parents you were born
And what can you give back to them that equals their gift
to you?
Ecclesiasticus 7.28 (Judaeo-Christian)

442 There has never been a man trained to benevolence who has
neglected his parents.
Mencius 1.1.1 (Confucianism)

443 Support your mother and father,
thus you will win this world.
Sutra-krit-anga I.3.2.4 (Jainism)

444 Whosoever being rich does not support mother and father
when old and past their youth, let one know him as an out-
cast.
Sutta Nipata 123 (Buddhism)

445 A wise son brings joy to his father,
but a foolish man despises his mother.
Proverbs 15.20 (Judaeo-Christian)

446 The parents of a child are but his enemies when they fail to
educate him properly in his boyhood.
Garuda Purana (Hinduism)

447 Give thanks to Me and to your parents.
Koran 31.13 (Islam)

448 Of all the men in the world
There are none equal to brothers.
Shih King (Confucianism)

449   Love your brother like your soul,
       and guard him like the pupil of your eye.
                    Gospel of Thomas II.38.10–12 (Gnosticism)

450   A family must begin to destroy itself before others will.
                    Mencius 4.1.8.4 (Confucianism)

451   A wife of noble character is her husband's crown,
       but a disgraceful wife is like decay in his bones.
                    Proverbs 12.4 (Judaeo-Christian)

452   The love of a faithful wife remains constant whatever the
       husband loses or wins.
                    Hitopadesa (Hinduism)

453   The world and all its things are valuable,
       but more valuable than all is a virtuous woman.
                    Mishkat-el-Masabih (Islam)

454   He who finds a wife finds what is good and receives favor
       from the Lord.
                    Proverbs 18.22 (Judaeo-Christian)

455   A virtuous wife is a man's greatest treasure.
                    Hadith 418 (Islam)

456   He who loves his wife as himself,
       honors her more than himself.
                    Talmud (Judaism)

457   From the loving example of one family a whole state becomes
       loving.
                    The Great Learning 9.3 (Confucianism)

458   Better to live on a corner of the roof than share a house with a
       quarrelsome wife.
                    Proverbs 21.9 (Judaeo-Christian)

459   Men ruin themselves by their search abroad while the real
      thing is in their homes.
                          Adi Granth (Sikhism)

460   Honor your wife and your life will be enriched.
                          Talmud (Judaism)

461   Husbands, love your wives,
         and do not be harsh with them.
                          Colossians 3.19 (Christianity)

462   He who has sons has delight in sons.
                          Sutta Nipata 32 (Buddhism)

463   He who educates his own son or the son of another,
         it is as though he educated the Son of God.
                          Gleanings from the
                          Writings of Baha'u'llah (Baha'i)

464   A daughter is a secret anxiety to her father,
         and the worry of her keeps him awake at night.
                          Ecclesiastes 42.9 (Judaeo-Christian)

465   He who has no son has no place in the world;
         in the person of a son a man is reborn,
         a second self is begotten.
                          Aitareya Brahmana 7.13 (Hinduism)

466   A man's home is his wife.
                          Talmud (Judaism)

467   Take care of your dear husband
         As though you served a god.
                          Mila Grubum (Buddhism)

468   Frequent repetition of the act of propagating the offspring is
         an act of great worth.
                          Avesta (Zoroastrianism)

469 Heaven lies at the feet of mothers.
Hadith 222 (Islam)

470 A wife's charm delights her husband,
and her skill puts fat on his bones.
Ecclesiasticus 26.13 (Judaeo-Christian)

FEAR

471 Do not fear the reproach of men or be terrified by their
insults.
Isaiah 51.7 (Judaeo-Christian)

472 Pitiful is the one who fearing failure,
makes no beginning.
Hitopadesa (Hinduism)

473 The sage does not fear for his life.
Sutra-krit-anga I.2.2.16 (Jainism)

474 Don't be afraid, just believe.
Mark 5.36 (Christianity)

475 To say "What all men fear I must fear" is pointless.
Tao Teh Ching 20 (Taoism)

476 So long as a man does not sin he is feared,
as soon as he sins he himself is in fear.
Talmud (Judaism)

477 Through remembrance of the Lord our fears are dispelled.
Sukhmani (Sikhism)

478 Do not be afraid of those who kill the body but cannot kill
the soul.
Matthew 10.28 (Christianity)

479 Know ye that I am afraid of none except God.
Gleanings from the
Writings of Baha'u'llah LXVI (Baha'i)

480 Fear him who, after the killing of the body,
has power to throw you into hell.
Luke 12.5 (Christianity)

481 Without fear love does not spring up nor does the mind
become pure.
Adi Granth (Sikhism)

482 Fear not; for, verily I am with you.
Koran 20.48 (Islam)

483 Blessed are all who fear the Lord,
who walk in his ways.
Psalms 128.1 (Judaeo-Christian)

484 To live in fear and falsehood is worse than death.
Menog-i Khrad 19.4 (Zoroastrianism)

485 If you are mired by fears and doubts,
you can't go forward.
I Ching 57.6 (Taoism)

486 The fear of the Lord teaches a man wisdom,
and humility comes before honor.
Proverbs 15.33 (Judaeo-Christian)

487 Once bitten, twice shy.
Jatakas 148 (Buddhism)

488 The fear of the Lord is the beginning of knowledge but fools
despise wisdom and discipline.
Proverbs 1.7 (Judaeo-Christian)

489 If, on examining himself, a man finds nothing to reproach
himself for, what worries and fears can he have?
Analects XII.4 (Confucianism)

490 Fear and evil rule the world,
       and only he who knows is saved.
                          Kirtan Sohila (Sikhism)

FOOL

491 Sand, salt, and a piece of iron are easier to bear than a stupid man.
                          Ecclesiasticus 22.15 (Judaeo-Christian)

492 There is no companionship with a fool.
                          Dhammapada 61 (Buddhism)

493 A sensible man is wiser than he knows,
       while a fool knows more than is wise.
                          Tao Teh Ching 81 (Taoism)

494 The mind of a fool is like a broken jar;
       it will hold no knowledge.
                          Ecclesiasticus 21.14 (Judaeo-Christian)

495 He is a fool who does not delight in liberality.
                          Dhammapada 177 (Buddhism)

496 Sad is the steadfastness with which the fool clings to his sloth, his sorrow, and his fears.
                          Bhagavad Gita 17 (Hinduism)

497 Better a poor man whose walk is blameless than a fool whose lips are perverse.
                          Proverbs 19.1 (Judaeo-Christian)

498 The wrong action seems sweet to the fool until the reaction comes and brings pain, and the bitter fruits of wrong deeds have then to be eaten.
                          Dhammapada 69 (Buddhism)

499   The fool thinketh that all is his own.
          Adi Granth (Sikhism)

500   The fool hath said in his heart, there is no God.
          Psalms 14.1 (Judaeo-Christian)

501   The fool waits for "lucky days,"
        but luck always misses him.
          Jatakas 49 (Buddhism)

502   The wise, through not thinking, become foolish.
          Shu King 5.18.2 (Confucianism)

503   Better to meet a bear robbed of its cubs than a fool in his folly.
          Proverbs 17.12 (Judaeo-Christian)

504   Fools may be big, but great they can never be.
          Dhammapada 202 (Buddhism)

505   We are not unquestionably sages;
        they are not unquestionably fools.
          Nihongi XXII (Shinto)

506   It is better to heed a wise man's rebuke,
        than to listen to the song of fools.
          Ecclesiastes 7.5 (Judaeo-Christian)

507   Women are to the foolish a temptation,
        difficult to resist.
          Sutra-krit-anga I.3.4.16 (Jainism)

508   To your heart this lesson take—
        fools suffer for their folly.
          Hitopadesa (Hinduism)

509   Like a thornbush in a drunkard's hand is a proverb in the
        hands of a fool.
          Proverbs 26.9 (Judaeo-Christian)

510   For one word a man is often deemed to be wise,
and for one word he is often deemed to be foolish.
Analects XIX.25 (Confucianism)

511   To shame the wise, God has chosen what the world counts
folly, and to shame what is strong.
1 Corinthians 1.27 (Christianity)

512   A man who knows that he is a fool is not a great fool.
Chuang-tzu XII (Taoism)

FORGIVING

513   When angry, forgive.
Koran 42.35 (Islam)

514   Be forgiving of others, taking no account of what they may
say about you.
Namdhari Rahit-nama (Sikhism)

515   If you forgive men when they sin against you,
your heavenly father will also forgive you.
Matthew 6.14 (Christianity)

516   Who does not forgive, is guilty of offence.
Rig Veda I.24.14 (Hinduism)

517   Do thou forgive with kindly forgiveness.
Koran 15.85 (Islam)

518   Bless those who curse you,
pray for those who mistreat you.
Luke 6.28 (Christianity)

519   Forgiveness is the strength of those who are endued with good qualities.
                    Mahabharata 5.39.71 (Hinduism)

520   He who does not forgive, is guilty of offense.
                    Mahavagga 1.21.4 (Buddhism)

521   He who has been forgiven little loves little.
                    Luke 7.47 (Christianity)

522   Where there is forgiveness, there is God himself.
                    Analects IV.2 (Confucianism)

523   He to who more is forgiven, loves more.
                    Logia (Christianity)

524   Anger must be conquered by forgiveness.
                    Mahabharata 5.39.73 (Hinduism)

525   Forgive your neighbor the hurt that he has done to you, so shall your sins also be forgiven when you pray.
                    Ecclesiasticus 28.2 (Judaeo-Christian)

526   Those who are willing to forget old grievances will gradually do away with resentment.
                    Analects V (Confucianism)

527   The most beautiful of all things man can do is to forgive wrong.
                    Rokeach (Judaism)

528   Where there is forgiveness, there is God himself.
                    Kabir's Sloks (Sikhism)

529   I forgive all souls: let all souls forgive me.
                    Avesyaka Sutra (Jainism)

530   Forgive, and you will be forgiven.
                    Luke 6.37 (Christianity)

FRIENDSHIP

531 A faithful friend is a sturdy shelter;
he that has found one has found a treasure.
Ecclesiasticus 6.14 (Judaeo-Christian)

532 Friendship and enmity are bound to each other by a distinct
chain of cause and effect.
Garuda Purana (Hinduism)

533 Do not accept as friend anyone who is not as good as you.
Analects I.8 (Confucianism)

534 The best friend is God.
Talmud (Judaism)

535 Foolish friends are worse than wise enemies.
Jatakas 44 (Buddhism)

536 A man does not repose so much confidence in his sons, wives
and brothers as he implicitly places in his own natural
friend.
Garuda Purana (Hinduism)

537 Forsake not an old friend,
for the new is not comparable unto him.
Ecclesiastes 9.10 (Judaeo-Christian)

538 Be a new friend to an old friend.
Pand Nameh I (Zoroastrianism)

539 The excellence of friendship is measured by love.
Tao Teh Ching 8 (Taoism)

540 A friend loves at all times,
and a brother is born for adversity.
Proverbs 17.17 (Judaeo-Christian)

541 Thou art thine own friend;
why wishest thou for a friend beyond thyself?
Acharanga Sutra I.3.3.4 (Jainism)

542   In this life there is none more happy than he who has a friend
to converse with, a friend to live with, and a friend to chat
with.
Hitopadesa (Hinduism)

543   Do not forget a friend in your heart,
and be not unminded of him in your wealth.
Ecclesiasticus 37.6 (Judaeo-Christian)

544   To converse with your friends is like cool water on the soul.
Intimate Conversations (Sufism)

545   Superior men extinguish the fire of hate by friendship.
Iti-vuttaka 93 (Buddhism)

546   A friend is like gold, and trials are like fire:
the pure gold is well and happy in the heart of the fire.
Masnavi (Sufism)

547   Be conscientious in speaking to your friend,
but tactful in your efforts to guide him aright.
Analects XII.23 (Confucianism)

548   A friend cannot be known in prosperity:
and an enemy cannot be hidden in adversity.
Ecclesiastes 12.8 (Judaeo-Christian)

549   He is the true friend who is beside us when trouble comes our
way.
Hitopadesa (Hinduism)

550   Friendship for a fool and love for a great man are like lines
drawn on water, which leave neither trace nor mark.
Asa Ki War 22 (Sikhism)

551   Have a great number of friends, but not counselors.
The Teachings
of Silvanus VII.97.18–19 (Gnosticism)

552 A gentleman makes friends through being cultivated,
     but looks to friends for support in benevolence.
                        Analects XII.24 (Confucianism)

553 There is no greater love than this,
     that a man should lay down his life for his friends.
                        John 15.13 (Christianity)

554 Requite evil with good, and he who is your enemy will
     become your dearest friend.
                        Koran 41.30 (Islam)

555 The friends who love you best are never afraid to speak the
     truth, no matter how painful or difficult it might be.
                        I Ching 39.5 (Taoism)

556 That man is a hero that can make a friend out of a foe.
                        Talmud (Judaism)

GIVING

557 Begin by giving alms to your own relatives.
                        Mishkat-el-Masabih (Islam)

558 A wise man should always share with others.
                        Mahabharata (Hinduism)

559 When you give to the needy, do not let your left hand know
     what your right hand is doing, so that your giving may be
     in secret.
                        Matthew 6.3-4 (Christianity)

560 Save thyself by giving; what's given is well saved.
                        Anguttara Nikaya 3.6.52 (Buddhism)

561 Charity without faith can never be the means of salvation.
Siri-siri-valaka 19 (Jainism)

562 He gives little who gives much with a frown;
he gives much who gives little with a smile.
Talmud (Judaism)

563 Woe to the giver who gives for the joy of his own soul.
Avesta (Zoroastrianism)

564 Gifts which are bestowed with kindness make the giving doubly dear.
Hitopadesa (Hinduism)

565 It is more blessed to give than to receive.
Acts 20.35 (Christianity)

566 He who relieves the poor, makes the Lord King.
Avesta (Zoroastrianism)

567 People give according to their faith or according to their pleasure.
Dhammapada 249 (Buddhism)

568 God loveth a cheerful giver.
2 Corinthians 9.7 (Christianity)

569 Gifts must be given in abundance, with joy, humility, and compassion.
Taittiriya Upanishad (Hinduism)

570 To be charitable in public is good, but to give alms to the poor in private is better and will atone for some of your sins.
Koran 2.271 (Islam)

571 Every good and perfect gift is from above.
James 1.17 (Christianity)

572   The beggar is worthy of the gift.
        Mahabharata (Hinduism)

573   Freely you have received, freely give.
        Matthew 10.8 (Christianity)

574   Whoso would merit win
    Long-lasting, bringing bliss—
  Let him give alms, be calmed,
    And cultivate good will.
        Iti-vuttaka 22 (Buddhism)

575   Great is the greatness of him who gives without being asked.
        Adi Granth (Sikhism)

576   For him that giveth, merit comes to growth.
        Udana VIII.5 (Buddhism)

577   Give, and it will be given to you.
        Luke 6.38 (Christianity)

578   You cannot give what you do not have.
        I Ching 44.4 (Taoism)

579   Give, and your wealth shall grow; give, and you shall the more safely keep the wealth you have.
        Hitopadesa (Hinduism)

580   Give to the one who asks you, and do not turn away from the one who wants to borrow from you.
        Matthew 5.42 (Christianity)

581   He who is granted the blessing of grace is the one who can know what it means.
        Adi Granth (Sikhism)

582   Wherefore, a man being evil cannot do that which is good; neither will he give a good gift.
        Moroni 7.10 (Mormonism)

583 When you have given gifts,
     help will come in the form of future wealth.
                         Bya Chos (Buddhism)

584 A gentleman gives to help the needy and not to maintain the
     rich in style.
                         Analects VI.4 (Confucianism)

585 The wicked borrow and do not repay,
     but the righteous give generously.
                         Psalms 37.21 (Judaeo-Christian)

586 Sometimes He gives while depriving you,
     and sometimes He deprives you in giving.
                         The Book of Wisdom 83 (Sufism)

587 You shall never be truly righteous until you give in alms what
     you dearly cherish.
                         Koran 3.92 (Islam)

588 He that giveth, let him do it with simplicity.
                         Romans 12.8 (Christianity)

589 Those whose pity and charity are wide will have their life
     extended immeasurably.
                         Oracle of Hachiman (Shinto)

590 To give and yet be checked by meanness
     —that prolongs the bondage.
                         Bya Chos (Buddhism)

591 A gift is pure when it is given from the heart to the right
     person at the right time and at the right place, and when
     we expect nothing in return.
                         Bhagavad Gita 17.20 (Hinduism)

GOD

592 All things are of God.
            2 Corinthians 5.18 (Christianity)

593 Know thyself and thou will know God.
            Hazrat Ali (Sufism)

594 Who denies God, denies himself.
         Who affirms God, affirms himself.
            Taittiriya Upanishad 2.6 (Hinduism)

595 The voice of the people is as the voice of God.
            Talmud (Judaism)

596 God dwelleth in everything, God shineth in every heart.
            Adi Granth (Sikhism)

597 He is not far from each one of us.
            Acts 17.27 (Christianity)

598 God leads men to tranquil security.
            Shu King 5.14 (Confucianism)

599 It is everywhere but everywhere it is nothing.
            Chuang-tzu VI (Taoism)

600 The world we see reflects God's form;
         when God grows it grows too.
            Sohar Rahiras (Sikhism)

601 Be pleasing to God, and you will not need anyone.
            The Teachings
            of Silvanus VII.98.18–20 (Gnosticism)

602 God upholds the oneness of this universe: the seen and the
         unseen, the transient and the eternal.
            Svetasvatara Upanishad I (Hinduism)

603 God is greater than our own hearts,
      and he knows everything.
                    1 John 3.20 (Christianity)

604 If you want to know me,
      look inside your heart.
                    Tao Teh Ching 70 (Taoism)

605 Perfected are the words of your Lord in truth and justice.
                    Koran 6.115 (Islam)

606 God is love; and he that dwelleth in love dwelleth in God,
      and God in him.
                    1 John 4.16 (Christianity)

607 He is ONE in all, but it seems as if he were many.
                    Bhagavad Gita 13.16 (Hinduism)

608 God is a principle which exists by virtue of its own intrin-
      sicality, and operates spontaneously, without self-manifes-
      tation.
                    Chuang-tzu (Taoism)

609 The foolishness of God is wiser than man's wisdom,
      and the weakness of God is stronger than man's strength.
                    1 Corinthians 1.25 (Christianity)

610 Thou didst truly create right,
      and art the Lord to judge the actions of life.
                    Yasna 31.8 (Zoroastrianism)

611 He is neither divided as a body,
      nor split up into the names which he has.
                    Tripartite Tractate I.66.37–39 (Gnosticism)

612 He who sees that the Lord of all is ever the same in all that
      is, immortal in the field of mortality—he sees the truth.
                    Bhagavad Gita 13.27 (Hinduism)

613 God is to be likened to whatever is loftiest.
                          Koran 16.62 (Islam)

614 The glory of God is intelligence.
                          Doctrine and Covenants (Mormonism)

615 No one was before he was,
              and no one has rule over him;
              because he is the source of all,
              and he is also the ruler of all.
                          Svetasvatara Upanishad VI (Hinduism)

616 In describing him there would never be an end.
                          Japji Granth (Sikhism)

617 He is sustenance;
              he is joy;
          He is truth;
              he is rejoicing;
          He is rest.
                          Tripartite Tractate I.55.15–17 (Gnosticism)

618 The Tao which can be expressed in words is not the eternal
          Tao; the name which can be uttered is not its eternal name.
                          Tao Teh Ching 1 (Taoism)

619 No eye has seen, no ear has heard, no mind has conceived
          what God has prepared for those who love him.
                          Isaiah 64.4 (Judaeo-Christian)

620 He has no beginning, no middle, no end;
              no past, no present, no future.
                          Dasam Granth (Sikhism)

621 The eyes do not see him, speech cannot utter him, the senses
          cannot reach him.
                          Mundaka Upanishad (Hinduism)

622   The more you talk about It,
       the more you think about It,
       the further from It you go.
                   On Trust in the Heart (Zen)

623   He who is loved by man is loved by God.
                   Talmud (Judaism)

624   Do not worry, but believe in God.
                   Gorikai (Shinto)

625   If men thought of God as much as they think of the world,
       who would not attain liberation.
                   Maitri Upanishad (Hinduism)

626   It flows through all things, inside and outside, and returns to
       the origin of all things.
                   Tao Teh Ching 25 (Taoism)

627   With God all things are possible.
                   Matthew 19.26 (Christianity)

628   The might of God is equal to all things.
                   Koran 33.27 (Islam)

629   By thinking, I cannot obtain a conception of him,
       even though I think hundreds of thousands of times.
                   Adi Granth (Sikhism)

630   If you lean on a staff of metal it will bend, and wood and
       bamboo will break, but if you take God for your staff all
       will be easy.
                   Gorikai (Shinto)

631   All that is and ever was comes from a God of knowledge.
                   The Manual of Discipline (Judaism)

632   All things issue from it; all things return to it.
                   Tao Teh Ching 52 (Taoism)

633 Nothing is, or can ever be, hidden from God.
Gleanings from the
Writings of Baha'u'llah (Baha'i)

634 In truth who knows God becomes God.
Mundaka Upanishad 3.2 (Hinduism)

635 Even in a single leaf of a tree, or a tender blade of grass, the
awe-inspiring deity manifests itself.
Urabe-no-Kanekuni (Shinto)

636 Commit to the Lord whatever you do,
and your plans will succeed.
Proverbs 16.3 (Judaeo-Christian)

637 Those who by my form did see me,
And those who followed me by my voice,
Wrong are the efforts they engaged in,
Me those people will not see.
Diamond Sutra (Buddhism)

638 The Spirit supreme is immeasurable, inapprehensible,
beyond conception, never-born, beyond reasoning,
beyond thought.
Maitri Upanishad (Hinduism)

639 Ye are children of the Lord your God.
Deuteronomy 14.1 (Judaeo-Christian)

640 Not one of the names which are conceived, spoken, seen, or
grasped, not one of them applies to him, even in they are
exceedingly glorious, great, and honored.
Tripartite Tractate I.54.2–8 (Gnosticism)

641 God is in the beginning, the middle, and the end, and none
besides is seen.
Adi Granth (Sikhism)

642   The word of God is living and active.
                 Hebrews 4.12 (Christianity)

643   One who knows what is of God patterns his living after God.
                 Chuang-tzu (Taoism)

644   God is in all which is in the truth.
                 The Teachings
                 of Silvanus VII.101.12 (Gnosticism)

645   Know that everything is vanity but God.
                 Mishkat-el-Masabih (Islam)

646   He is neither manifest nor hidden,
         He is neither revealed nor unrevealed:
      There are no words to tell that which He is.
                 Songs of Kabir IX (Sikhism)

647   He is knowledge and the object of knowledge.
                 Bhagavad Gita 13.17 (Hinduism)

648   God is the keeper of heaven and earth:
         separation from him is impossible.
                 Gorikai (Shinto)

649   God sees everyone; no one looks at him.
                 The Teachings
                 of Silvanus VII.101.15–17 (Gnosticism)

650   Wherever I look, there is God, no one else is seen.
                 Adi Granth (Sikhism)

651   He is the light of all lights and luminous beyond all the
      darkness of our ignorance.
                 Bhagavad Gita 13.17 (Hinduism)

652   The capacity to connect with the spirit of wisdom,
         to imagine in one's heart-mind—
         this is how God becomes known.
                 Zohar (Kabbalah)

653 If God is for us, who can be against us?
Romans 8.31 (Christianity)

654 As the web issues from the spider, as little sparks proceed
from fire, so from the one soul proceed all breathing
animals, all worlds, all the gods, and all beings.
Brihad-Aranyaka Upanishad (Hinduism)

655 For I am the one who alone exists,
and I have no one who will judge me.
The Thunder, Perfect Mind VI.21.18–20
(Gnosticism)

GOLDEN RULE

656 That nature alone is good which shall not do unto another
whatever is not good for its own self.
Dadistan-i-Dinik XCIV.5 (Zoroastrianism)

657 Do nothing to thy neighbor which hereafter thou wouldst
not have thy neighbor do to thee.
Mahabharata (Hinduism)

658 Lay not on any soul a load which ye would not wish to be
laid upon you.
Gleanings from the
Writings of Baha'u'llah LXVI (Baha'i)

659 Love your enemies, and pray for those who persecute you.
Matthew 5.44 (Christianity)

660 Honest men never injure the wicked,
even if injured by them.
Mahabharata 1.74.93 (Hinduism)

661   That which one desireth not for oneself,
         do not do unto others.
                        The Staff of Wisdom (Buddhism)

662   Indifferent to worldly objects, a man should wander about
         treating all creatures in the world so as he himself would
         be treated.
                        Sutra-krit-anga (Jainism)

663   Love your neighbor as yourself.
                        Luke 10.30 (Christianity)

664   No one of you is a believer until he loves for his brother what
         he loves for himself.
                        Hadith (Islam)

665   When abused, do not abuse.
                        Mahabharata (Hinduism)

666   Regard your neighbor's gain as your own gain:
         and regard your neighbor's loss as your own loss.
                        T'ai Shang Kan Ying P'ien (Taoism)

667   Do not repay anyone evil for evil.
                        Romans 12.17 (Christianity)

668   Do unto all men as you would they should do unto you, and
         reject for others what you would reject for yourself.
                        Mishkat-el-Masabih (Islam)

669   As one's life is dear to himself,
         so also are those of all beings.
                        Hitopadesa (Hinduism)

670   Do not impose on others what you yourself do not desire.
                        Analects XII.2 (Confucianism)

671   Hurt not others with that which pains yourself.
                        Udana V.18 (Buddhism)

672   Treat others as thou wouldst be treated thyself.
Adi Granth (Sikhism)

673   All Comrades who do not love one another divert themselves from the straight path.
Zohar (Kabbalah)

674   Do not unto others all that which is not well for oneself.
Shayast-na-shayast 13.29 (Zoroastrianism)

675   A considerate man will always cultivate
In act, thought and speech
That which is good for living beings.
Vishnu Purana 3.12.45 (Hinduism)

676   Desire not for anyone the things that ye would not desire for
yourselves.
Gleanings from the
Writings of Baha'u'llah LXVI (Baha'i)

677   Do to others what you would have them do to you.
Matthew 7.12 (Christianity)

678   Never do to others what would pain thyself.
Panchatantra III.104 (Hinduism)

679   What is hurtful to yourself do not to your fellow man.
Talmud (Judaism)

GOOD

680   Let us do good to all people.
Galatians 6.10 (Christianity)

681   He that does good, does it for his own soul;
          and he that commits evil does so at his own peril.
                        Koran 41.44 (Islam)

682   It's the good who honor the good in the world,
          The wicked never obtain a good mind.
                        Mahabharata (Hinduism)

683   Seek good, not evil, that you may live.
                        Amos 5.14 (Judaeo-Christian)

684   Desiring one's own good,
          One should reject the four vices:
          Namely, wrath, vanity, fraud, and greed.
                        Dasaveyaliya 8.37 (Jainism)

685   What is a good man but a bad man's teacher?
                        Tao Teh Ching 27 (Taoism)

686   Depart from evil and do good; seek peace and ensue it.
                        First Epistle of Clement
                        to the Corinthians 11.4 (Christianity)

687   If you do good, you do it for your own souls;
          if you do evil, you do it to yourself.
                        Koran 17.7 (Islam)

688   Dedicate yourself to thinking about and doing good.
                        Tibetan Book of the Dead (Buddhism)

689   Turn from evil and do good;
          then you will always live securely.
                        Psalms 37.27 (Judaeo-Christian)

690   A gentleman can do nothing greater than to encourage men
          to do good.
                        Mencius 2.1.8 (Confucianism)

691   Good it is to do the good deed which brings no remorse.
                        Dhammapada 314 (Buddhism)

692 Do not be overcome with evil,
  but overcome evil with good.
  Romans 12.21 (Christianity)

693 Do good for evil.
  Adi Granth (Sikhism)

694 All are good at first,
  but few prove themselves to be so at the last.
  Shu King 3.1.7–8 (Confucianism)

695 Do not withhold good from those who deserve it, when it is
  in your power to act.
  Proverbs 3.27 (Judaeo-Christian)

696 Ever and always one should be doing good.
  Bhagavad Gita 6.40 (Hinduism)

697 I am not good, nor do I find anyone bad.
  Adi Granth (Sikhism)

698 The good man brings up good things out of the good stored
  up in him.
  Matthew 12.35 (Christianity)

699 Blessed is the man who speaketh what is good,
  who thinketh what is good,
  who practiseth what is good.
  T'ai-Shang Kan Ying P'ien (Taoism)

700 Blessed are they that choose the good;
  they that choose the pleasant miss the goal.
  Katha Upanishad (Hinduism)

701 The opportunities for doing good may never fail.
  Talmud (Judaism)

702 Holiness is the best of all good.
  Avesta (Zoroastrianism)

703 It is easy to do what is wrong, to do what is bad for oneself;
but very difficult to do what is right, to do what is good for
oneself.
Dhammapada 163 (Buddhism)

704 He that is good shall be rewarded with what is better.
Koran 28.83 (Islam)

705 He who seeks good finds good will,
but evil comes to him who searches for it.
Proverbs 11.27 (Judaeo-Christian)

GREED

706 The stingy man pays the highest price.
Tao Teh Ching 44 (Taoism)

707 Indulge in no excessive greed.
Panchatantra II (Hinduism)

708 Be content with what you have.
Hebrews 13.5 (Christianity)

709 The superior seeks what is right;
the inferior one, what is profitable.
Analects IV (Confucianism)

710 The holder of a monopoly is a sinner and offender.
Mishkat-el-Masabih (Islam)

711 The miser who hides his treasure in the earth opens up a
passage for his soul to sink into hell.
Hitopadesa (Hinduism)

712 Hell and destruction are never full;
so the eyes of man are never satisfied.
Proverbs 27.20 (Judaeo-Christian)

713   There is no greater calamity than indulging in greed.
Tao Teh Ching 46 (Taoism)

714   Greed is the mind's pollution,
falsehood pollutes the tongue.
Asa Ki War (Sikhism)

715   Whoever loves money never has money enough;
whoever loves wealth is never satisfied with his income.
Ecclesiastes 5.10 (Judaeo-Christian)

716   A rash and foolish man, forgetting that his life will have an
end, is full of selfishness.
Sutra-krit-anga I.10.18 (Jainism)

717   From four to eight, from thence to sixteen,
and so on to thirty-two,
insatiated greed goes on and on.
Dhammapada 369 (Buddhism)

718   A greedy man stirs up dissension.
Proverbs 28.35 (Judaeo-Christian)

719   He who gives up greed becomes happy.
Mahabharata (Hinduism)

720   By the thirst for riches the foolish man destroys himself as if
he were his own enemy.
Dhammapada 355 (Buddhism)

721   Better one handful with tranquility than two handfuls with
toil and chasing after the wind.
Ecclesiastes 4.6 (Judaeo-Christian)

722   Greed brings woe,
while contentment is all happiness.
The Sayings of Sri Ramakrishna (Hinduism)

723   Avidity is boundless like space.
                    Uttara-Dhyayana Sutra 9.17 (Jainism)

724   Greed is the real dirt, not dust;
          Greed is the term for real dirt.
      The wise have shaken off this dirt,
          And in the dirt-free man's religion live.
                    Visuddhimagga XII (Buddhism)

725   He who loves silver shall not be satisfied with silver, nor he
      who loves abundance, with increase.
                    Ecclesiastes 5.11 (Judaeo-Christian)

726   Where there is greed, what love can there be?
                    Adi Granth (Sikhism)

HAPPINESS

727   True happiness consists in making happy.
                    Bharavi's Kiratarjuniya 7.28 (Hinduism)

728   Happiness is a disease the remedy for which is unhappiness.
                    Adi Granth (Sikhism)

729   He who for the sake of happiness hurts others who also want
      happiness, shall not hereafter find happiness.
                    Dhammapada 131 (Buddhism)

730   Happy is he who has found wisdom,
          and the man who has acquired understanding.
                    Proverbs 3.13 (Judaeo-Christian)

731   Liberty or emancipation is the only happiness vouchsafed to
      man.
                    Garuda Purana (Hinduism)

732   To be fond of something is better than merely to know it, and
       to find joy in it is better than merely to be fond of it.
       Analects VI.20 (Confucianism)

733   There is no riches above a sound body,
       and no joy above the joy of the heart.
       Ecclesiasticus 30.16 (Judaeo-Christian)

734   He who leads a regular life, having understood what is good,
       and penetrated the truth, will obtain happiness.
       Sutta Nipata 322 (Buddhism)

735   Happy is the man who is holy with perfect holiness.
       Avesta (Zoroastrianism)

736   Ask and you will receive, and your joy will be complete.
       John 16.24 (Christianity)

737   True happiness lies in the extinction of all emotions.
       Garuda Purana (Hinduism)

738   Be always studious to be in harmony with the ordinances of
       God, and you will obtain much happiness.
       Mencius 4 (Confucianism)

739   Chastity is the parent of human happiness.
       The Ocean of Delight for the Wise (Buddhism)

740   There is no happiness without devotion to God.
       Adi Granth (Sikhism)

741   With coarse food to eat, water to drink, and a bent arm for a
       pillow, happiness may still be found.
       Analects VII (Confucianism)

742   Weeping may remain for a night,
       but rejoicing comes in the morning.
       Psalms 30.5 (Judaeo-Christian)

743   The greatest happiness is having tranquility of mind.
Subhashita Ratna Nidhi (Buddhism)

744   If your happiness depends on money,
you will never be happy with yourself.
Tao Teh Ching 44 (Taoism)

745   Men, like cats,
are ever ready to pounce upon happiness.
Garuda Purana (Hinduism)

746   The happiness of the impious and the unhappiness of the
righteous are incomprehensible things.
Talmud (Judaism)

747   No soul knoweth what joy is reserved for the good in recompense of their works.
Koran 32.17 (Islam)

748   It is not easy to find a man who after three years of self-
cultivation has not reached happiness.
Analects VIII.12 (Confucianism)

749   Those free from idleness alone derive supreme enjoyment.
Samaveda III.3 (Hinduism)

750   It is good to tame the mind and to guard one's thoughts; a
tamed mind and thoughts well guarded bring happiness.
Dhammapada 35–36 (Buddhism)

751   To be in accord with man, is human happiness.
To be in accord with God, is the happiness of God.
T'ai Shang Kan Ying P'ien (Taoism)

752   True happiness consists in self-reliance.
Laws of Manu 4.160 (Hinduism)

753   He who conquers himself through himself will obtain happiness.
Uttara-Dhyayana Sutra 9.35 (Jainism)

754 Joy and gladness shall be yours, as you school yourself by day
and by night in the things that are right.
Majjhima Nikaya 1.417 (Buddhism)

755 Happiness is to be found in contentment.
Tao Teh Ching 33 (Taoism)

HATRED

756 Victory breeds hatred,
for the conquered is ill at ease.
Dhammapada 201 (Buddhism)

757 If the world hates you,
keep in mind that it hated me first.
John 15.18 (Christianity)

758 Do not profess love with your lips while you harbor hatred
in your heart.
Gorikai (Shinto)

759 A religionist, if beaten, should never be angry.
Uttara-Dhyayana Sutra 2.26 (Jainism)

760 Unrighteous anger cannot be justified,
for a man's anger tips the scale to his ruin.
Ecclesiasticus 1.22 (Judaeo-Christian)

761 Clothe not thy heart with anger.
Adi Granth (Sikhism)

762 There is no losing throw like hatred.
Dhammapada 202 (Buddhism)

763 Requite hatred with goodness.
Tao Teh Ching 63 (Taoism)

764 In wrath remember mercy.
Habakkuk 3.2 (Judaeo-Christian)

765 As the jasmine sheds its wilted flowers,
even so man should shed lust and hatred.
Dhammapada 377 (Buddhism)

766 A wise man should not be angry, when reprimanded.
Uttara-Dhyayana Sutra 1.9 (Jainism)

767 Against an angry man, be not angry.
Laws of Manu 6.48 (Hinduism)

768 Refrain from anger and turn away from wrath;
do not fret—it leads only to evil.
Psalms 37.8 (Judaeo-Christian)

769 He who, by causing pain to others, wishes to obtain pleasure
for himself, will become entangled in bonds of hatred and
will never be free from hatred.
Dhammapada 291 (Buddhism)

770 Do not bring bitterness to your own heart by anger at the
things that are past.
Gorikai (Shinto)

771 Let not hatred towards any induce you to do wrong.
Koran 5.11 (Islam)

772 When the wise is angry he is wise no longer.
Talmud (Judaism)

773 For a man quick with a retort there are frequent occasions on
which he will incur the hatred of others.
Analects V.5 (Confucianism)

774 Anger in a wise man is never justified.
Jatakas 351 (Buddhism)

775 Let not the sun go down upon your wrath.
Ephesians 4.26 (Christianity)

776 Hatred is not diminished by hatred at any time.
Hatred is diminished by love —
this is the eternal law.
Dhammapada 5 (Buddhism)

THE HEART

777 As he thinketh in his heart, so is he.
Proverbs 23.7 (Judaeo-Christian)

778 A merciful, tender heart is the seed of love.
Mencius 2.1.6 (Confucianism)

779 There is a light that shines beyond all things on earth,
beyond us all, beyond the heavens, beyond the highest,
beyond the very highest heavens. This is the light that
shines in our heart.
Chandogya Upanishad (Hinduism)

780 A cheerful heart is good medicine.
Proverbs 17.22 (Judaeo-Christian)

781 Many millions search for God and find him in their hearts.
Adi Granth (Sikhism)

782 Out of men's hearts come evil thoughts, sexual immorality,
theft, murder, adultery, greed, malice, deceit, lewdness,
envy, slander, arrogance, and folly.
Mark 7.21–22 (Christianity)

783 Both heaven and hell come from one's own heart.
Kojiki (Shinto)

784   The heart is deceitful above all things,
and desperately wicked.
Jeremiah 17.9 (Judaeo-Christian)

785   The heart of a man is more dangerous than mountains and
rivers, more difficult to understand than heaven itself.
Chuang-tzu XXXII (Taoism)

786   That which is needed most is a loving heart.
Fo-Sho-Hing-Tsan-King 1032 (Buddhism)

787   He in whose heart there is jealousy, shall never prosper.
Adi Granth (Sikhism)

788   Freedom from bonds is in your innermost heart.
Acharanga Sutra (Jainism)

789   For where your treasure is,
there your heart will be also.
Matthew 6.21 (Christianity)

790   Attach not to thy heart lust, wrath, covetousness, obstinacy
and worldly love.
Adi Granth (Sikhism)

791   If a man sets his heart on benevolence,
he will be free from evil.
Analects IV.4 (Confucianism)

792   An obstinate heart shall be laden with sorrow.
Ecclesiasticus 3.27 (Judaeo-Christian)

793   Set not thy heart on mansions and wealth.
Sloks of Shaikh Farid (Sikhism)

794   The best preacher is the heart.
Talmud (Judaism)

795 All men have hearts,
    and each heart has its own leaning.
           Nihongi XXII (Shinto)

796 As water reflects a face,
    so a man's heart reflects the man.
           Proverbs 27.19 (Judaeo-Christian)

797 Man's sins are the work of his heart.
           Kabir's Sloks 101 (Sikhism)

798 So long as the heart of man is directed towards God,
    he cannot be lost in the ocean of worldliness.
           The Sayings of Sri Ramakrishna (Hinduism)

799 Each heart knows its own bitterness,
    and no one else can share its joy.
           Proverbs 14.10 (Judaeo-Christian)

800 The heart in sleep becomes a window.
           Masnavi 1508 (Sufism)

801 The instructor, the learner, the hearer and the enemy are
    always within the heart.
           Anugita 2.17 (Hinduism)

802 A godly heart produces a blessed life.
           The Sentences of Sextus XII.28.22–23
           (Gnosticism)

803 Man is born according to the desires of his heart,
    and he is absorbed in the same way.
           Adi Granth (Sikhism)

804 A happy heart makes the face cheerful,
    but heartache crushes the spirit.
           Proverbs 15.13 (Judaeo-Christian)

805   The spiritual gain of a person depends upon his sentiments and ideas, proceeds from his heart and not from his visible actions.
The Sayings of Sri Ramakrishna (Hinduism)

806   If my eyes are asleep,
still my heart is not asleep.
Hadith (Islam)

807   The heart carries the feet.
Talmud (Judaism)

808   One should not speak sincerity with his mouth and lack sincerity in his heart.
Gorikai (Shinto)

809   When all the ties that bind the heart are unloosened, then a mortal becomes immortal.
Katha Upanishad VI (Hinduism)

810   The heart that loves is always young.
Talmud (Judaism)

HUMILITY

811   All is vanity.
Ecclesiastes 3.19 (Judaeo-Christian)

812   He who gives up vanity is loved by all.
Mahabharata (Hinduism)

813   If you desire to obtain help, put away pride.
Oracle of the Gods of Kasuga (Shinto)

814   Proclaim your virtues in a whisper,
       and your faults in a loud voice.
                        Talmud (Judaism)

815   People praise you for what they suppose is in you;
       but you must blame your soul for what you know is in it.
                 The Book of Wisdom 142 (Sufism)

816   For whoever exalts himself will be humbled;
       and whoever humbles himself will be exalted.
                    Matthew 23.12 (Christianity)

817   The gentleman is at ease without being arrogant;
       the small man is arrogant without being at ease.
                  Analects XIII.26 (Confucianism)

818   See that ye are not lifted up unto pride;
          yea, see that ye do not boast in your own wisdom,
       nor of your much strength.
                     Alma 38.11 (Mormonism)

819   He who is contented with contentment shall always be con-
       tent.
                   Tao Teh Ching 46 (Taoism)

820   When pride comes, then comes disgrace,
       but with humility comes wisdom.
                 Proverbs 11.2 (Judaeo-Christian)

821   He comes to ruin who says that others are not equal to
       himself.
                 Shu King 4.2.4 (Confucianism)

822   Humility is an abomination to a proud man.
                Ecclesiasticus 13.20 (Judaeo-Christian)

823   Humility is the root of honor;
       lowliness, the foundation of loftiness.
                   Tao Teh Ching 39 (Taoism)

824 The earth does not talk, but all things prosper.
Hekiganroku 47 (Zen)

825 A man's pride brings him low,
but a man of lowly spirit gains.
Proverbs 29.23 (Judaeo-Christian)

826 A man improves himself by humility when he rises in rank
by his wealth and good deeds.
Dinkard VIII.447 (Zoroastrianism)

827 A superior man is ashamed of a reputation beyond his merits.
Mencius 4.2.18 (Confucianism)

828 Let another praise you, and not your own mouth.
Proverbs 27.2 (Judaeo-Christian)

829 Those who aspire to greatness,
must humble themselves.
Tao Teh Ching 61 (Taoism)

830 Be humble before all men.
The Sayings of the Fathers 4.12 (Judaism)

831 Though fearless, be modest.
Sutra-krit-anga I.14.22 (Jainism)

832 God sets his face against the arrogant but favors the humble.
1 Peter 5.5 (Christianity)

833 Humility and courtesy are acts of piety.
Hadith 84 (Islam)

834 Man has been created on the last day,
even the gnat is of a more ancient lineage.
Talmud (Judaism)

835 Who knows of what he is created is saved from pride.
The Song of the Dervish (Sufism)

836   In humility, consider others better than yourselves.
                    Philippians 2.3 (Christianity)

837   Standing tiptoe a man loses balance,
          Walking astride he has no pace,
      Kindling himself he fails to light,
          Acquitting himself he forfeits his hearers,
      Admiring himself he does so alone.
                    Tao Teh Ching 24 (Taoism)

838   Modesty is the best policy.
                    I Ching 15.4 (Taoism)

839   Modesty is a branch of faith.
                    Mishkat-el-Masabih (Islam)

840   By myself I can do nothing.
                    John 5.30 (Christianity)

841   And when spiritual knowledge manifests itself,
          Do not make much of yourselves by a willingness to talk.
                    Mila Grubum (Buddhism)

842   Begging is a hard task.
                    Sutra-krit-anga I.3.1.6 (Jainism)

843   Humility and the fear of the Lord bring wealth and honor
      and life.
                    Proverbs 22.4 (Judaeo-Christian)

844   Even if your eye is like a shooting star,
          and your spirit like lightning,
          you are still like the turtle,
          which cannot avoid dragging its tail.
                    Hekiganroku 24 (Zen)

845   Humility is the word,
          forbearance the virtue,
          civility the priceless spell.
                    Adi Granth (Sikhism)

846   My lowliness is my exaltation,
and my exaltation is my lowliness.
Talmud (Judaism)

847   Let him that is humble, not bear witness to himself,
but let him leave it to another to bear witness of him.
First Epistle of Clement
to the Corinthians 17.37 (Christianity)

848   He who deemeth himself lowly shall be deemed the most
exalted of all.
Adi Granth (Sikhism)

849   Humility in oneself is as correct as grandeur among inferiors.
Dadistan-i dinik 1.11 (Zoroastrianism)

850   Pride goes before destruction,
a haughty spirit before a fall.
Proverbs 16.18 (Judaeo-Christian)

851   Do not think yourself so large as to deem others small.
Shu King 4.6.4 (Confucianism)

JUDGMENT

852   If we judged ourselves,
we would not come under judgment.
1 Corinthians 11.31 (Christianity)

853   Let a man continually take pleasure in justice.
Laws of Manu 4.175 (Hinduism)

854   I tell you judges, you have been judged.
The Second Apocalypse
of James V.57.20–22 (Gnosticism)

855   Hasty judgment shows no man just.
Dhammapada 256 (Buddhism)

856   Stop judging by mere appearances,
and make a right judgment.
John 7.24 (Christianity)

857   Give full measure, when you measure, and weigh with even
scales.
Koran 17.35 (Islam)

858   Judge not alone, for none may judge alone save One.
The Sayings of the Fathers 4.10 (Judaism)

859   There are varying grades with God:
and God beholdeth what ye do.
Koran 3.157 (Islam)

860   The Lord abhors dishonest scales,
but accurate weights are his delight.
Proverbs 11.1 (Judaeo-Christian)

861   True is the Lord, true his decision,
True the justice He meteth out as an example.
Hymns of Guru Nanak (Sikhism)

862   We generally reproach others with blemishes similar to our
own.
Talmud (Judaism)

863   Only those skilled in meditation are thus free to judge wisely.
Tibetan Book of the Dead (Buddhism)

864   Let a man continually take pleasure in justice.
Laws of Manu 4.175 (Hinduism)

865   See that ye do not judge wrongfully; for with that same judgment which ye judge ye shall also be judged.
Moroni 7.18 (Mormonism)

866   Don't criticize other people's faults,
         criticize your own.
                        Analects V (Confucianism)

867   Whatever measure you deal out to others will be dealt back
         to you.
                        Matthew 7.2 (Christianity)

868   To strive for purity of vision, and yet be blinded by a faulty
         judgment—that prolongs the bondage.
                        Bya Chos (Buddhism)

869   In judging your fellow-man you condemn yourself,
         since you, the judge, are equally guilty.
                        Romans 2.1 (Christianity)

870   The things which long ago were decreed
         Shall in eternity overcome wickedness with justice.
                        Yasna 48.1 (Zoroastrianism)

871   Do not put maliciousness in your judgment,
         for every malicious man harms his heart.
                        The Teachings
                        of Silvanus VII.97.3–6 (Gnosticism)

872   Rather than base one's judgment on the opinions of the
         many, let each one look after his own affairs.
                        Chuang-tzu (Taoism)

873   Why do you look at the speck of sawdust in your brother's
         eye and pay no attention to the plank in your own?
                        Matthew 7.3 (Christianity)

874   Be fair in your judgment.
                        Gleanings from the
                        Writings of Baha'u'llah CXIII (Baha'i)

875   Judge not, and ye shall not be judged.
                        Luke 6.37 (Christianity)

KNOWLEDGE

876 The more knowledge, the more life.
>The Sayings of the Fathers 2.8 (Judaism)

877 The greatest gift is the gift of knowledge.
>Bhagavata Purana (Hinduism)

878 Without stepping outside one's doors,
one can know what is happening in the world.
>Tao Teh Ching 47 (Taoism)

879 The simple inherit folly,
but the prudent are crowned with knowledge.
>Proverbs 14.18 (Judaeo-Christian)

880 The energetic rags of knowledge create supreme felicity for
the dynamic soul, which it cherishes internally.
>Samaveda VII.1.3 (Hinduism)

881 There is a limit to our life;
but to knowledge there is no limit.
>Chuang-tzu III.1 (Taoism)

882 When a wise man is instructed, he gets knowledge.
>Proverbs 21.11 (Judaeo-Christian)

883 I do not say that the attainment of gnosis comes straight-
away, but that it comes by a gradual training, a gradual
practice, a gradual course.
>Majjhima Nikaya I.479–80 (Buddhism)

884 How can it be known that what I call knowing is not really
not knowing and that what I call not knowing is not really
knowing?
>Chuang-tzu (Taoism)

885 I was not born with knowledge but,
being fond of antiquity, I am quick to seek it.
Analects VII.20 (Confucianism)

886 Knowledge imparted is knowledge gained.
Garuda Purana (Hinduism)

887 Knowledge is the most grievous veil between man and his
Creator.
The Book of Certitude 69 (Baha'i)

888 Through knowledge shall the just be delivered.
Proverbs 11.9 (Judaeo-Christian)

889 In me (knowledge) be the fulfillment of all thy wishes.
Yajurveda XII.46 (Hinduism)

890 Bodily pleasure or pain does not belong to him who possesses
absolute knowledge.
Pravacana-sara 1.20 (Jainism)

891 The best knowledge is the one accompanied by fear.
The Book of Wisdom 232 (Sufism)

892 A man who knows how little he knows is well,
A man who knows how much he knows is sick.
Tao Teh Ching 71 (Taoism)

893 Knowledge is the best treasure that a man can secretly hoard
up in life.
Garuda Purana (Hinduism)

894 I know nothing by myself.
1 Corinthians 4.4 (Christianity)

895 Those who know do not tell,
those who tell do not know.
Tao Teh Ching 56 (Taoism)

896 Let him who desires knowledge be taught the holy word.
                 Avesta (Zoroastrianism)

897 Make divine knowledge thy food.
                 Japji Granth 29 (Sikhism)

898 The fixtures and furniture of one's house may be stolen by
            thieves; but knowledge, the highest treasure, is above all
            stealing.
                 Garuda Purana (Hinduism)

899 Seek knowledge from the cradle to the grave.
                 Hadith 274 (Islam)

900 What man knows is not to be compared with what he does
            not know.
                 Chuang-tzu XVII (Taoism)

901 He who knows both knowledge and action,
            with action overcomes death
            and with knowledge reaches immortality.
                 Isha Upanishad (Hinduism)

902 The Father of knowledge
            Is the Word of Knowledge.
                 The Odes of Solomon 7.7 (Christianity)

903 A little knowledge is a dangerous thing.
                 Chuang-tzu (Taoism)

904 Knowledge and love of God are ultimately one and the same.
                 The Sayings of Sri Ramakrishna (Hinduism)

905 Whatever principle of intelligence we attain unto in this life,
            it will rise with us in the resurrection.
                 Doctrine and Covenants 130.18 (Mormonism)

LANGUAGE

906 By your words you will be acquitted,
and by your words you will be condemned.
Matthew 12.37 (Christianity)

907 Better than a thousand useless words is one single word that
gives peace.
Dhammapada 100 (Buddhism)

908 [May] the right time precede your words.
The Sentences of Sextus XII.15.4 (Gnosticism)

909 Straight words seem crooked.
Tao Teh Ching 78 (Taoism)

910 He puts his words into action before allowing his words to
follow his action.
Analects II.13 (Confucianism)

911 Speech is the messenger of the heart.
Talmud (Judaism)

912 Swayed by words, one is lost;
Blocked by phrases, one is bewildered.
Mumonkan 37 (Zen)

913 When words are many, sin is not absent,
but he who holds his tongue is wise.
Proverbs 10.19 (Judaeo-Christian)

914 But in so far as one is free from words
Does one really understand words.
Saraha's Treasury of Songs 88 (Buddhism)

915 Artful words will ruin one's virtue.
Analects XV.27 (Confucianism)

916   The more the words, the less the meaning,
        and how does that profit anyone?
                    Ecclesiastes 6.11 (Judaeo-Christian)

917   Words which give peace, words which are good and beautiful
        and true, and also the reading of sacred books: this is the
        harmony of words.
                    Bhagavad Gita 17.15 (Hinduism)

918   A word is sufficient to the wise,
        as a flick of the whip is to a fine horse.
                    Hekiganroku 70 (Zen)

919   Put thy cleverness away:
        mere words shall never unite thee to him.
                    Songs of Kabir LIX (Sikhism)

920   A word aptly spoken is like apples of gold in settings of silver.
                    Proverbs 25.11 (Judaeo-Christian)

921   A kind word with forgiveness is better than charity followed
        by insult.
                    Koran 2.263 (Islam)

922   The whole world is tormented by words
        And there is no one who does without words.
                    Saraha's Treasury of Songs 58 (Buddhism)

923   Do not imagine that words are sufficient to raise us to heaven
        or save us from hell.
                    Adi Granth (Sikhism)

924   For that which goes into your mouth will not defile you, but
        that which issues from your mouth – it is that which will
        defile you.
                    Gospel of Thomas II.35.24–27 (Gnosticism)

925   He should not tell anything sinful, meaningless or hurtful,
        neither for his own sake, nor for anybody else's.
                    Uttara-Dhyayana Sutra 1.25 (Jainism)

926 Shun profane and vain babblings:
for they will increase unto more ungodliness.
2 Timothy 2.16 (Christianity)

927 The gentleman does not recommend a man on account of
what he says, neither does he dismiss what is said on account of the speaker.
Analects XV.23 (Confucianism)

928 Do not answer before you have heard,
nor interrupt a speaker in the midst of his words.
Ecclesiasticus 11.8 (Judaeo-Christian)

929 Words cannot express things;
Speech does not convey the spirit.
Mumonkan 37 (Zen)

930 He who misappropriates, misapplies, and mismanages speech,
mismanages everything.
Laws of Manu 4.256 (Hinduism)

931 The tongue has the power of life and death,
and those who love it will eat its fruit.
Proverbs 18.21 (Judaeo-Christian)

932 The tongue is a smoldering fire,
and excess of speech a deadly poison.
The Book of Certitiude 193 (Baha'i)

933 If anyone considers himself religious and yet does not keep a
tight rein on his tongue, he deceives himself and his
religion is worthless.
James 1.26 (Christianity)

934 If you chatter on and on,
You will find you have lost your way.
Mumonkan 24 (Zen)

935   [If you speak] after [many (others) you will see] more the
     disadvantage.
                    The Sentences of Sextus XII.15.26–27
                    (Gnosticism)

936   If there be one, a wise man, fain of speech,
     He knows the proper time, and speech concerned
     With righteousness and practice of right talk.
                    Anguttara-Nikaya 199 (Buddhism)

937   Reckless words pierce like a sword,
     but the tongue of the wise brings healing.
                    Proverbs 12.18 (Judaeo-Christian)

938   When to act is difficult,
     is it any wonder that one is loath to speak?
                    Analects XII.3 (Confucianism)

939   Talking too much spoils your virtue;
     Silence is truly unequaled.
                    Mumonkan 27 (Zen)

940   Truthful lips endure forever,
     but a lying tongue lasts only a moment.
                    Proverbs 12.19 (Judaeo-Christian)

941   One should speak truth, and speak what is pleasant;
     one should not speak unpleasant truth:
     one should not speak pleasant falsehood.
                    Laws of Manu (Hinduism)

942   Great speech is universal,
     small speech is particular.
                    Chuang-tzu (Taoism)

943   An honest answer is like a kiss on the lips.
                    Proverbs 24.26 (Judaeo-Christian)

944 Those who recite commentaries do not know how to cleanse the world.
Saraha's Treasury of Songs 51 (Buddhism)

945 It is enough that the language one uses gets the point across.
Analects XV.41 (Confucianism)

946 Speak for pleasure, speak with measure,
Speak with grammar's richest treasure,
Not too much, and with reflection —
Deeds will follow words' direction.
Panchatantra III (Hinduism)

LEADERSHIP

947 The common people can be made to follow a path but not to understand it.
Analects VIII.9 (Confucianism)

948 Handle a large kingdom with as gentle a touch as if you were cooking small fish.
Tao Teh Ching 60 (Taoism)

949 When wise men are entrusted with office,
the sound of praise arises.
Nihongi XXII (Shinto)

950 If a blind man leads a blind man,
both will fall into a pit.
Matthew 15.14 (Christianity)

951 The best king is he whose countrymen live under him without fear, like sons in the house of their father.
Mahabharata (Hinduism)

952   If you want to learn how to govern,
          avoid being clever or rich.
                    Tao Teh Ching 65 (Taoism)

953   It is difficult to be a ruler,
          and it is not easy to be a subject, either.
                    Analects XIII.15 (Confucianism)

954   A leader is best
          When people barely know that he exists,
          Not so good when people obey and acclaim him,
          Worst when they despise him.
                    Tao Teh Ching 17 (Taoism)

955   Whosoever will be chief among you,
          let him be your servant.
                    Matthew 20.27 (Christianity)

956   The wise should know the law.
                    Acharanga Sutra I.6.4.2 (Jainism)

957   Be proud and you will never lead.
                    Tao Teh Ching 24 (Taoism)

958   Do not concern yourself with matters of government unless
          they are the responsibility of your office.
                    Analects VIII.14 (Confucianism)

959   The good shepherd lays down his life for the sheep.
                    John 10.11 (Christianity)

960   If you want to govern the people,
          you must place yourself below them.
          If you want to lead the people,
          you must learn how to follow them.
                    Tao Teh Ching 66 (Taoism)

961   Authority buries those who assume it.
                    Talmud (Judaism)

962   When one by force subdues men,
          they do not submit to him in heart.
                              Mencius 2 (Confucianism)

963   A ruler who oppresses the poor is like a driving rain that
          leaves no crops.
                              Proverbs 28.3 (Judaeo-Christian)

964   If a ruler be not able to love men,
          he cannot possess his own person.
                              Li Ki 7.4.8 (Confucianism)

965   The path that a great man follows becomes a guide to the
          world.
                              Bhagavad Gita 3.21 (Hinduism)

966   Ceremonies and laws are the lowest form of government.
                              Chuang-tzu (Taoism)

967   A tyrannical ruler lacks judgment.
                              Proverbs 28.16 (Judaeo-Christian)

968   Good government is feared by the people,
          while good instructions are loved by them.
                              Mencius 7 (Confucianism)

969   The best leader follows the will of the people.
                              Tao Teh Ching 68 (Taoism)

970   If a king judges the poor with fairness,
          his throne will always be secure.
                              Proverbs 29.14 (Judaeo-Christian)

971   Encourage the people to work hard by setting an example
          yourself.
                              Analects XIII.1 (Confucianism)

972   The horse curses the rider.
                              Avesta (Zoroastrianism)

973 Rule by love.
Mencius 1.2.12 (Confucianism)

LOVE

974 Love rules willing hearts; fear, the unwilling.
Logia (Christianity)

975 When love is firmly established in his heart, a man becomes master of himself and a teacher of humanity.
Bhagavata Purana (Hinduism)

976 Love is patient; love is kind and envies no one.
1 Corinthians 13.1 (Christianity)

977 Have compassion upon all creatures.
Uttara-Dhyayana Sutra 14.32 (Jainism)

978 Love without rebuke is no love.
Talmud (Judaism)

979 If you love others but are not loved in return examine your own feeling of benevolence.
Mencius 4.1.4 (Confucianism)

980 All beside love is but words.
Selections from the Writings
of Abdu'l Baha (Baha'i)

981 Let your love be without pretense.
Romans 12.9 (Christianity)

982 Love cannot be outnumbered.
Mencius 4.1.7 (Confucianism)

983   Only by love can men see me,
     and know me, and come unto me.
Bhagavad Gita 11.54 (Hinduism)

984   Do everything in love.
1 Corinthians 16.14 (Christianity)

985   To lack love, when nothing hinders us, is to lack wisdom.
Mencius 2.1.7 (Confucianism)

986   Faith receives, love gives.
Gospel of Phillip II.61.36 (Gnosticism)

987   They love not who live in counting the favors and frowns of
     love.
Adi Granth (Sikhism)

988   To love a thing makes the eye blind, the ear deaf.
Talmud (Judaism)

989   Pain has its root in love or affection.
Garuda Purana (Hinduism)

990   Do not love the world or anything in the world.
1 John 2.15 (Christianity)

991   When love renounces all limits, it reaches truth.
Songs of Kabir L (Sikhism)

992   Hatred stirs up dissension,
     but love covers over all wrongs.
Proverbs 10.12 (Judaeo-Christian)

993   There is no difference between pure knowledge and pure
     love.
The Sayings of Sri Ramakrishna (Hinduism)

994   Knowledge puffs up, but love builds up.
1 Corinthians 8.1 (Christianity)

995 Fruitless is that knowledge which is not love.
Bhagavata Purana (Hinduism)

996 Whoever does not love does not know God,
because God is love.
1 John 4.8 (Christianity)

997 More than all else do I cherish at heart that love which
makes me to live a limitless life in this world.
Songs of Kabir XXIV (Sikhism)

998 The love of man is the beginning of godliness.
The Sentences of Sextus XII.32.16–17
(Gnosticism)

999 Real love is neither diminished by unkindness,
nor increased by kindness.
Yahya (Sufism)

1000 Love your neighbor as yourself.
Leviticus 19.18 (Judaeo-Christian)

1001 There are three kinds of love,
—unselfish, mutual, and selfish.
The Sayings of Sri Ramakrishna (Hinduism)

1002 Let us love one another,
for love comes from God.
1 John 4.7 (Christianity)

1003 Fall in love in order to be somebody.
The Song of the Dervish (Sufism)

1004 Love is as strong as death.
Song of Solomon 8.6 (Judaeo-Christian)

1005 In truth, the lover is the one who spends generously on you,
not the one on whom you spend generously.
The Book of Wisdom 243 (Sufism)

1006   He who loves his fellow man has fulfilled the law.
Romans 13.8 (Christianity)

1007   Blessed is he who mingleth with all men in a spirit of utmost
kindliness and love.
Gleanings from the
Writings of Baha'u'llah 334 (Baha'i)

1008   Love one another.
John 13.34 (Christianity)

1009   Love the world as your self;
then you can care for all things.
Tao Teh Ching 13 (Taoism)

1010   Let us not love with words or tongue,
but with actions and truth.
1 John 3.18 (Christianity)

1011   It is better to love than to hate.
Tibetan Book of the Dead (Buddhism)

1012   Better is open rebuke than hidden love.
Proverbs 27.5 (Judaeo-Christian)

1013   Vain indeed is all struggle for spiritual life if in one's heart
there be not love.
Bhagavata Purana (Hinduism)

1014   There is nothing love cannot face.
1 Corinthians 13.7 (Christianity)

LUST

1015   The fruit of lust is pain and toil.
Bhagavad Gita 14 (Hinduism)

1016   As rain breaks through an ill-thatched roof,
        so lust breaks through an ill-thatched mind.
                Dhammapada 13 (Buddhism)

1017   The one who sows to please his sinful nature,
        from that nature will reap destruction.
                Galatians 6.8 (Christianity)

1018   When a man dwells on the pleasures of sense,
        attraction for them arises in him.
                Bhagavad Gita 2.62 (Hinduism)

1019   Knowledge is never coupled with lust of the world,
        if you desire the angel, cast out the dog.
                Gulshan-i-raz (Sufism)

1020   If you crave for pleasures
        Your troubles but increase.
                Mila Grubum (Buddhism)

1021   If men's passions are deep, their divinity is shallow.
                Chuang-tzu (Taoism)

1022   A pleasure-(loving) man is useless [in everything].
                The Sentences of Sextus XII.16.13–14
                (Gnosticism)

1023   Never surrender to carelessness;
        never sink into weak pleasures and lust.
                Dhammapada 27 (Buddhism)

1024   Passion, being kin to appetite, and breeding impulse and
        propensity, binds the embodied soul.
                Bhagavad Gita 14 (Hinduism)

1025   The sinful nature desires what is contrary to the spirit.
                Galatians 5.17 (Christianity)

1026   The hunger of passions is the greatest disease.
Dhammapada 202 (Buddhism)

1027   The only end of man is enjoyment produced by sensual pleasures.
Sarva-Darsana-Samgraha (Hinduism)

1028   O lust, thou givest an abode in hell,
thou causest man to wander in many a womb.
Adi Granth (Sikhism)

1029   The pleasure of wild sensuousness, of idleness,
and of indulgent feasting, are detrimental.
Analects XVI (Confucianism)

1030   Happy is freedom from lust in this world.
Mahavagga 1.3.4 (Buddhism)

1031   He who loves pleasure will become poor.
Proverbs 21.17 (Judaeo-Christian)

1032   Erroneous [thoughts] come because of the passions; when correct [thoughts] come the passions are cast aside.
Tan Ching 36 (Zen)

1033   Men who are pursued by lust run around like a hunted hare.
Dhammapada 342 (Buddhism)

1034   The slave to his lusts has forfeited human life and divine life.
Uttara-Dhyayana-Sutra 7.17 (Jainism)

1035   Woe to you who love intimacy with womankind and polluted intercourse with it.
The Book of Thomas
the Contender II.144.8–10 (Gnosticism)

1036   The eye and the tongue can commit adultery.
Hadith 15 (Islam)

1037 Anyone who looks at a woman lustfully has already com-
mited adultery with her in his heart.
Matthew 5.28 (Christianity)

1038 Burn sensual craving, make ink with its ashes,
as paper prepare heart and mind.
Adi Granth (Sikhism)

1039 Pain and pleasure are allied.
Hitopadesa (Hinduism)

MANKIND

1040 Let it be known that mankind is one,
that all men belong to a single humanity.
Dasam Granth (Sikhism)

1041 Mankind was but one people.
Koran 2.209 (Islam)

1042 The disease of men is this:
that they neglect their own fields
and go to weed the fields of others,
and that what they require from others is great,
while what they lay upon themselves is light.
Mencius 7.2.32 (Confucianism)

1043 Man is My mystery, and I am his mystery.
Gleanings from the
Writings of Baha'u'llah XC (Baha'i)

1044 Those who follow that part of themselves which is great are
great men; those who follow that part which is little are
little men.
Mencius (Confucianism)

1045   Man cometh in the course of nature and goeth in the course of nature.

> Adi Granth (Sikhism)

1046   Every man at his best state is altogether vanity.

> Psalms 39.5 (Judaeo-Christian)

1047   As a building supported by stout pillars on becoming old, falls into ruins, so man subject to age, must one day meet with dissolution.

> Ramayana (Hinduism)

1048   Though differences seem to mark and distinguish, all men are in reality the same.

> Dasam Granth (Sikhism)

1049   There is not a righteous man on earth who does what is right and never sins.

> Ecclesiastes 7.20 (Judaeo-Christian)

1050   Regard man as a flock of sheep that need a shepherd for their protection.

> Gleanings from the
> Writings of Baha'u'llah CLIX (Baha'i)

1051   Man is born for uprightness.

> Analects VI.17 (Confucianism)

1052   Men have walked both in wisdom and in folly.

> The Manual of Discipline (Judaism)

1053   Man, like a brute beast addicted only to animal gratification, suffers the pain that ignorance brings about.

> Vishnu Purana (Hinduism)

1054   Man at his best, like water,
        Serves as he goes along:
   Like water he seeks his own level,
        The common level of life.

> Tao Teh Ching 8 (Taoism)

1055   A man who has riches without understanding is like the
       beasts that perish.
                           Psalms 49.20 (Judaeo-Christian)

1056   In eating, sleeping, fearing, and copulating,
          men and beasts are alike;
       Man excelleth the beast by engaging
          in religious practices.
       So why should a man, if he be without religion,
          not be equal to the beast?
                           The Staff of Wisdom (Buddhism)

1057   The worst of men is a bad learned man;
          and the best of men is a good learned man.
                           Hadith 269 (Islam)

1058   A man should always be soft as a reed and not hard like a
       cedar.
                           Talmud (Judaism)

1059   Man indeed is this Universe,
          What has been, and what is to come,
       Master of immortality,
          When he rises through nourishment.
                           Rig Veda X.90.2 (Hinduism)

1060   All men are brothers;
          all receive the blessings of the same heaven.
                           Munetada (Shinto)

1061   A man whose mind is set on high ideals never forgets that
       he may end up in a ditch; a man of valour never forgets
       that he may forfeit his head.
                           Mencius (Confucianism)

1062   In a place where there is no man,
          strive to be a man.
                           Talmud (Judaism)

1063   As the fields are damaged by weeds,
         mankind is damaged by lust, hatred, and delusion.
                        Dhammapada 356 (Buddhism)

1064   Man is begotten by his father and instructed by his teacher.
                        Li Ki (Confucianism)

1065   God hath made of one blood all nations of men.
                        Acts 17.26 (Christianity)

1066   The purpose of God in creating man hath been, and will
         ever be, to enable him to know his Creator and attain his
         presence.
                        Gleanings from the
                        Writings of Baha'u'llah 334 (Baha'i)

1067   Man is the product of the attributes of heaven and earth.
                        Li Ki 7.3.1 (Confucianism)

1068   Men appear in two classes: one says exertion consists in
         works, and the other, in abstention from works.
                        Sutra-krit-anga I.8.2 (Jainism)

1069   Man is born to trouble as sure as sparks fly upward.
                        Job 5.7 (Judaeo-Christian)

1070   I see no other single hindrance such as this hindrance of
         ignorance, obstructed by which mankind for a long long
         time runs on and circles on.
                        Iti-vuttaka (Buddhism)

1071   Why should you stand in fear of man,
         when you are all immortal?
                        Mahabharata (Hinduism)

1072   Man is like a breath;
         his days are like a fleeting shadow.
                        Psalms 144.4 (Judaeo-Christian)

1073   Let a wise man remove impurities from himself even as a silversmith removes impurities from the silver: one after one, little by little, again and again.
                    Dhammapada 239 (Buddhism)

1074   I have yet to meet the man who is as fond of virtue as he is of beauty in women.
                    Analects IX.18 (Confucianism)

1075   The man without anger surpasses the angry,
          The man of forgiveness the unforgiving,
          And over the animals man stands first,
          And over the ignorant stand the wise.
                    Mahabharata (Hinduism)

1076   As iron sharpens iron,
          so one man sharpens another.
                    Proverbs 27.17 (Judaeo-Christian)

1077   Let man reflect from what he is created.
                    Koran 86.1 (Islam)

THE MIND

1078   Remember that your mind is so free that the slightest thought has great influence.
                    Tibetan Book of the Dead (Buddhism)

1079   It is not mind which we should want to know:
          we should know the Thinker.
                    Kaushitaki Upanishad (Hinduism)

1080   I know what is going through your mind.
                    Ezekiel 11.5 (Judaeo-Christian)

1081   The Mind like a mirror is brightly illuminating
           and knows no obstructions,
         It penetrates the vast universe to its minutest
           crevices;
         All its contents, multitudinous in form, are
           reflected in the mind,
         Which, shining like a perfect gem, has no surface,
           nor the inside.
                       Song of Enlightenment (Zen)

1082   The mind of man is of two kinds, pure and impure:
           impure when in the bondage of desire,
           pure when free from desire.
                       Maitri Upanishad (Hinduism)

1083   The mind's self-possession is only obtained by the senses
           being perfectly satisfied.
                       Buddha-Karita VII (Buddhism)

1084   While the essence of the mind is eternally clean and pure,
           the influence of ignorance makes possible the existence of
           a defiled mind.
                       The Awakening of Faith (Buddhism)

1085   The mind of those who sin in thought is impure.
                       Sutra-krit-anga I.1.2.29 (Jainism)

1086   Enlightenment is the highest quality of the mind.
                       The Awakening of Faith (Buddhism)

1087   It is the mind that makes one wise or ignorant, bound or
           emancipated.
                       The Sayings of Sri Ramakrishna (Hinduism)

1088   A man's own mind has sometimes a way of telling him more
           than seven watchmen posted high on a tower.
                       Ecclesiastes 37.14 (Judaeo-Christian)

1089　When one is well practised, the mind is held and does not run astray but remains fixed.
Shrichakrasambhara Tantra (Buddhism)

1090　In the mind are rising fast, resplendent waves of thought, wherein we bow before God.
Samaveda VII.1.2 (Hinduism)

1091　All that we say and whatever we hear is profitless wind if our minds are corrupt.
Adi Granth (Sikhism)

1092　If a man speaks or acts with a pure mind, joy follows him as his own shadow.
Dhammapada 2 (Buddhism)

1093　Mind is indeed the source of bondage and also the source of liberation.
Maitri Upanishad (Hinduism)

1094　When one's mind is cleansed,
Then one's master's good qualities may enter the heart.
Saraha's Treasury of Songs 39 (Buddhism)

1095　To a mind that is "still," the whole universe surrenders.
Chuang-tzu XIII (Taoism)

1096　It is bondage when the mind desires or grieves at anything, rejects or accepts anything, feels happy or angry at anything.
Ashtavakra Gita (Hinduism)

1097　To be carnally minded is death;
but to be spiritually minded is life and peace.
Romans 8.6 (Christianity)

1098　Know that wherever there is space there is consciousness.
Tibetan Book of the Dead (Buddhism)

1099   We would approach thee, God,
          with the help of thy good mind.
                    Yasna 36.4 (Zoroastrianism)

1100   They who have their minds under control never come to
          grief.
                    Mahabharata (Hinduism)

1101   When the mind ceases thus to be mind,
          The true nature of the Innate shines forth.
                    Saraha's Treasury of Songs (Buddhism)

1102   The sinful mind is hostile to God.
                    Romans 8.7 (Christianity)

1103   Whoever has a contented mind has all riches.
                    Hitopadesa (Hinduism)

1104   Whatever pours forth from the mind,
          Possesses the nature of the owner.
                    Saraha's Treasury of Songs 72 (Buddhism)

1105   Be ye all of one mind.
                    1 Peter 3.8 (Christianity)

1106   Better to emancipate your mind than your body;
          When the mind is emancipated, the body is free.
                    Mumonkan 9 (Zen)

1107   An enemy can hurt a enemy,
          and a man who hates can harm another man;
          but a man's own mind, if wrongly directed,
          can do him a far greater harm.
                    Dhammapada 42 (Buddhism)

1108   All men have a mind which cannot bear to see the suffering
          of others.
                    Mencius 2 (Confucianism)

1109   All mind is woven with the sense;
         but in a pure mind shines the light of the Self.
                     Mundaka Upanishad III.1 (Hinduism)

1110   What we are comes from our thoughts of yesterday,
         and our present thoughts build our life of tomorrow:
         our life is the creation of our mind.
                     Dhammapada 2 (Buddhism)

MODERATION

1111   In governing men and in serving heaven,
         there is nothing like moderation.
                     Tao Teh Ching 59 (Taoism)

1112   Drunkards and gluttons become poor,
         and drowsiness clothes them in rags.
                     Proverbs 23.21 (Judaeo-Christian)

1113   There is little to choose between overshooting the mark and
         falling short of it.
                     Analects XI.16 (Confucianism)

1114   Restraint in all things is good.
                     Mahavagga 5.1.16 (Buddhism)

1115   Add to your faith virtue, and to virtue knowledge, and to
         knowledge temperance.
                     2 Peter 1.5–6 (Christianity)

1116   Do not go to excess in pleasure.
                     Shu King 2.2.1 (Confucianism)

1117   Wine is a mocker and beer a brawler;
         whoever is led astray by them is not wise.
                     Proverbs 20.1 (Judaeo-Christian)

1118   There is no sin in eating meat, in drinking spirituous liquor, and in carnal intercourse, for that is the way of created beings, but abstention brings great rewards.
Laws of Manu (Hinduism)

1119   When an experiment as regards its being good is tried, so that having drunk it in that proportion one becomes better, or does not become worse, then it is allowable to drink it.
Dadistan-i-Dinik II.51 (Zoroastrianism)

1120   Wine and women will make men of understanding fall away.
Ecclesiasticus 19.2 (Judaeo-Christian)

1121   He who does not know his limit
And acts above his station,
Is as stupid as a fool.
Mila Grubum (Buddhism)

1122   Pleasures should not be carried to excess.
Li Ki 1.1.1.2 (Confucianism)

1123   Too much is always a curse, most of all in wealth.
Chuang-tzu XXIX (Taoism)

1124   Eat, ye, and drink; but exceed not;
for, He loveth not those who exceed.
Koran 7.29 (Islam)

1125   Go not too far, but learn to shun excess,
for overblowing lost what blowing won.
Jatakas 60 (Buddhism)

1126   Overstep not the bounds of moderation.
Gleanings from the
Writings of Baha'u'llah CXIV (Baha'i)

1127   Let your moderation be known unto all men.
Philippians 4.5 (Christianity)

1128   The superior man, when eating,
craves not to eat to the full.
Analects I (Confucianism)

1129   Seeking more when you are already full brings harm.
I Ching 27.2 (Taoism)

1130   Be not too straight nor too crooked.
Garuda Purana (Hinduism)

1131   Like a city whose walls are broken down is a man who lacks
self-control.
Proverbs 25.28 (Judaeo-Christian)

1132   A pious man eats little, drinks little, sleeps little.
Sutra-krit-anga I.8.25 (Jainism)

1133   Eat little, sleep little, love mercy and forbearance.
Gobind Singh (Sikhism)

1134   The wise reject all extremes.
Tao Teh Ching 29 (Taoism)

1135   When entertained by another with food and drink, eat not
too much, drink not too much.
Jatakas 477 (Buddhism)

1136   Wine is like life to men, if you drink it in moderation.
Ecclesiasticus 31.27 (Judaeo-Christian)

1137   To take all one wants is never as good as to stop when one
should.
Tao Teh Ching 9 (Taoism)

PARADOX

1138   There is nothing right that can truly be called right.
Hekiganroku 84 (Zen)

1139   There is nothing which is not *this*;
there is nothing which is not *that*.
Chuang-tzu (Taoism)

1140   He who knows one thing, knows all things;
and he who knows all things, knows one thing.
Acharanga Sutra (Jainism)

1141   Many who are first will be last,
and many who are last will be first.
Matthew 19.20 (Christianity)

1142   The farther one pursues knowledge, the less one knows.
Tao Teh Ching 47 (Taoism)

1143   When one sees Eternity in things that pass away and
Infinity in finite things,
then one has pure knowledge.
Bhagavad Gita 18.20 (Hinduism)

1144   There is nothing more visible than what is secret,
and nothing more manifest than what is minute.
Doctrine of the Mean (Confucianism)

1145   If you see through this moment's thought,
You see through the man who sees through this moment.
Mumonkan 47 (Zen)

1146   The Sage knows without running about,
Understands without seeing,
Accomplishes without doing.
Tao Teh Ching 47 (Taoism)

1147   That which you see is not:
and for that which is, you have no words.
Songs of Kabir XLIX (Sikhism)

1148   How can he be called filial who obeys his father when he is
commanded to do wrong?
Book of Filial Piety (Confucianism)

1149   There is nothing which is not objective:
there is nothing which is not subjective.
Chuang-tzu (Taoism)

1150   Women have one man in their heart, another in their
words, and still another in their arms.
Sutra-krit-anga I.4.1.16 (Jainism)

1151   My strength is made perfect in weakness.
2 Corinthians 12.9 (Christianity)

1152   A man naturally shuns a woman who loves him and is easily
available to him, and covets one whose touch is the forfeit
of life.
Garuda Purana (Hinduism)

1153   The rest in rest is not the real rest;
there can be rest even in movement.
Saikondan (Taoism)

1154   Perfection is an imperfection.
Tao Teh Ching 45 (Taoism)

1155   Below is like above.
The Odes of Solomon (Christianity)

1156   Any image that does not embrace male and female is not a
high and true image.
Zohar (Kabbalah)

1157   Nothing is absolutely right,
  and nothing is absolutely wrong.
    Chuang-tzu (Taoism)

1158   What is twisted cannot be straightened,
  what is lacking cannot be counted.
    Ecclesiastes 1.15 (Judaeo-Christian)

1159   Sometimes a man attains heaven, sometimes he goes to hell,
  and sometimes a dead man reaps both heaven and hell.
    Markandeya Purana (Hinduism)

1160   Separation is the same as construction;
  construction is the same as destruction.
    Chuang-tzu (Taoism)

1161   He alone possesses knowledge who knows that he knows
  nothing.
    Talmud (Judaism)

1162   The greatest cleverness appears like stupidity;
  the greatest eloquence seems like stuttering.
    Tao Teh Ching 65 (Taoism)

1163   Lunatics, drunkards and children sometimes give out the
  truth unconsciously, as if inspired by heaven.
    The Sayings of Sri Ramakrishna (Hinduism)

PERCEPTION

1164   It is not the failure of others to appreciate your abilities that
  should trouble you, but rather your own lack of them.
    Analects XIV.30 (Confucianism)

1165   For quarrelling, each to his view, they cling,
Such folk see only one side of a thing.
Udana VI.4 (Buddhism)

1166   What goes into a man's mouth does not make him unclean,
but what comes out of his mouth,
that is what makes him unclean.
Matthew 15.11 (Christianity)

1167   The wise man who can see far into the past and the future
will practice indifference.
Sutra-krit-anga I.2.2.4 (Jainism)

1168   You can tell those who are above average about the best,
but not those who are below average.
Analects VI.21 (Confucianism)

1169   There is nothing true anywhere
The true is nowhere to be seen;
If you say you see the true,
This seeing is not the true one.
Tan Ching (Zen)

1170   Recognize what is in your sight, and that which is hidden
from you will become plain to you.
Gospel of Thomas II.33.10–13 (Gnosticism)

1171   Regard external objects as being only visible and apparently
true, but having no independent and absolute reality in
themselves.
Shrichakrasambhara Tantra (Buddhism)

1172   Each tree is recognized by its own fruit.
Luke 6.44 (Christianity)

1173   Dream is one level
Vision is one level
Prophecy is one level.
Zohar (Kabbalah)

1174   Do not like, do not dislike;
        all then will be clear.
                    On Trust in the Heart (Zen)

1175   Be ever hearing, but never understanding;
        be ever seeing, but never perceiving.
                    Isaiah 6.9 (Judaeo-Christian)

1176   There is no difference between a temple or a mosque,
        nor between the prayer of a Hindu or a Muslim.
                    Dasam Granth (Sikhism)

1177   You don't ask a blind man's opinion of beautiful designs,
        nor do you invite a deaf man to a concert.
                    Chuang-tzu (Taoism)

1178   A blind man, though he may carry a light, still does not see.
                    Sutra-krit-anga I.12.8 (Jainism)

1179   Present a sword if you meet a swordsman;
        Don't offer a poem unless you meet a poet.
                    Mumonkan 33 (Zen)

1180   God endowed woman with more intelligence than man.
                    Talmud (Judaism)

1181   If you do not understand the minds of others,
        Never slander others or condemn their views.
                    Mila Grubum (Buddhism)

1182   He who looks on another's wife as a mother,
        on another's goods as a clod of earth,
        and on all creatures as himself, is a wise man.
                    Hitopadesa (Hinduism)

1183   And all things being equal, how can one say which is long
        and which is short.
                    Chuang-tzu (Taoism)

1184 It is not the failure of others to appreciate your abilities that should trouble you, but rather your failure to appreciate theirs.

> Analects I.16 (Confucianism)

POSSESSIONS

1185 You cannot receive understanding except you know first that you possess nothing.

> The Sentences of Sextus XII.29.12–14
> (Gnosticism)

1186 Ye, and all ye possess, shall pass away.

> Gleanings from the
> Writings of Baha'u'llah CXVI (Baha'i)

1187 And His possession is immortal life,
And those who receive it are incorruptible.

> The Odes of Solomon 40.6 (Christianity)

1188 When one loves one's possessions,
to lose them is a greater grief.

> Mahabharata (Hinduism)

1189 He who is the master of possessions is the slave of passions.

> Issac of Ninevah (Christianity)

1190 If you realize that all things change,
there is nothing you will try to hold on to.

> Tao Teh Ching 74 (Taoism)

1191 For we brought nothing into this world,
and it is certain we can carry nothing out.

> 1 Timothy 6.7 (Christianity)

1192 If one acquires possessions, all hell besets him:
the craving for riches is a greater grief—
if one has riches, it grows worse.
Mahabharata (Hinduism)

1193 Sell your possessions and give to the poor.
Luke 12.33 (Christianity)

1194 Music and fine clothes are the lowest form of happiness.
Chuang-tzu (Taoism)

1195 A man's life does not consist in the abundance of his possessions.
Luke 12.15 (Christianity)

1196 For the man who forsakes all desires and abandons all pride of possession and of self reaches the goal of peace supreme.
Bhagavad Gita 2.71 (Hinduism)

1197 Do not store up for yourselves treasures on earth, where moth and rust destroy, and where thieves break in and steal.
Matthew 6.19 (Christianity)

1198 If you want to be given everything, give everything up.
Tao Teh Ching 22 (Taoism)

1199 Is it not necessary for all those who possess everything to know themselves?
Gospel of Phillip II.76.17–19 (Gnosticism)

PRAYER

1200 Better is a little prayer with devotion than much without it.
Talmud (Judaism)

1201   Ritual prayer is a purification for hearts and an opening-up
       of the door of the invisible domains.
         The Book of Wisdom 119 (Sufism)

1202   He who offends against heaven has none to whom he can
       pray.
         Analects III.13 (Confucianism)

1203   The prayer of a righteous man is powerful and effective.
         James 5.16 (Christianity)

1204   Pray neither with too loud a voice nor in silence,
         but seek between these extremes a middle course.
         Koran 17.110 (Islam)

1205   Know that through prayer remembering comes, then rec-
       ognition, then acceptance, then at-oneness, then final
       liberation.
         Tibetan Book of the Dead (Buddhism)

1206   If you believe,
         you will receive whatever you ask for in prayer.
         Matthew 21.22 (Christianity)

1207   Prayers will be answered only if sincere.
         I Ching 46.2 (Taoism)

1208   If that which is within is not bright,
         it is useless to pray for that which is without.
         Oracle of Tatsuta (Shinto)

1209   The Lord is far from the wicked but he hears the prayer of
       the righteous.
         Proverbs 15.29 (Judaeo-Christian)

1210   Woe to those who pray but are heedless in their prayer; who
       make a show of piety and give no alms to the destitute.
         Koran 107.7 (Islam)

1211 If you pray to the deity with sincerity,
          you will assuredly realize the divine presence.
                    Chucho-Jijitsu (Shinto)

1212 Pray without ceasing.
                    1 Thessalonians 5.17 (Christianity)

1213 When prayer fails to help you accomplish your purpose,
          know that something is lacking in your sincerity.
                    Gorikai (Shinto)

1214 I make prayer mine inmost friend.
                    Atharva Veda VII.100 (Hinduism)

1215 When you pray turn your eyes downward and your heart
          upward.
                    Talmud (Judaism)

1216 Make truth thy prayer, faith thy prayer carpet.
                    Adi Granth (Sikhism)

1217 Do not approach your prayers when you are drunk,
          but wait till you can grasp the meaning of your words.
                    Koran 4.43 (Islam)

1218 We direct our prayers to thee with confessions of our guilt.
                    Yasna 36.5 (Zoroastrianism)

1219 He who makes his voice heard during prayer is small in
          faith.
                    Talmud (Judaism)

1220 The key to Paradise is prayer;
          and the key to prayer is ablution.
                    Hadith 354 (Islam)

1221 When you pray, go into your room, close the door and pray
          to your Father, who is unseen.
                    Matthew 6.6 (Christianity)

1222   When the world is in distress it heartily prayeth.
           Adi Granth (Sikhism)

1223   He who prays for his neighbor will be heard for himself.
           Talmud (Judaism)

1224   By praises and hymns one obtains the wisdom consisting in
           knowledge, faith, and conduct.
           Uttara-Dhyayana Sutra XXIX.14 (Jainism)

1225   Man prays for evil as fervently as he prays for good.
           Koran 17.12 (Islam)

1226   Prayer is worship in the heart.
           Talmud (Judaism)

QUEST

1227   Reveal thy simple self,
               Embrace thy original nature,
           Check thy selfishness,
               Curtail thy desires.
               Tao Teh Ching 19 (Taoism)

1228   Pleasure when young, gain in middle-age,
           and virtue in the end of life.
               Mahabharata 3.33.41 (Hinduism)

1229   A wise man, knowing the nature of excessive pride and
           deceit, giving them up all, brings about his liberation.
               Sutra-krit-anga (Jainism)

1230   Do not worry about people not knowing you,
           but strive so that you may be worth knowing.
               Analects V (Confucianism)

1231   The man who can be saved is the one who seeks after him
        and his mind and who finds each of them.
                    Zostrianos VIII.44.1–4 (Gnosticism)

1232   Energy, forgiveness, fortitude, purity, a good will, freedom
        from pride—these are the treasures of the man who is
        born for heaven.
                    Bhagavad Gita 16.3 (Hinduism)

1233   The man who does the will of God lives forever.
                    1 John 2.17 (Christianity)

1234   If you are intent on your spiritual welfare, do not kill any
        living being by your acts, by your orders, or by your con-
        sent.
                    Sutra-krit-anga I.2.3.21 (Jainism)

1235   Make thine own self pure, oh righteous man; every man in
        the world below can win purity for himself, by cleansing
        his heart with good thoughts, good words, and good
        deeds.
                    Avesta (Zoroastrianism)

1236   By faith the flood is crossed,
            By diligence the sea;
        By vigour ill is passed;
            By wisdom cleansed is he.
                    Milindapanha 35–36 (Buddhism)

1237   It is by grace you have been saved.
                    Ephesians 2.8 (Christianity)

1238   By knowledge one knows things.
            By faith one believes in them.
        By conduct one gets freedom.
            And by austerities one reaches purity.
                    Uttara-Dhyayana Sutra 2.10–13 (Jainism)

1239 Not to commit any sin, to do good, to purify one's mind:
      That is the teaching of all the awakened.
                    Dhammapada 183 (Buddhism)

1240 He who stands firm to the end will be saved.
                    Matthew 24.13 (Christianity)

1241 Forsake flesh and self and will, and cling to the One Truth
      of Heaven and Earth.
                    Kojiki (Shinto)

1242 When you see a good man, try to emulate his example, and
      when you see a bad man, search yourself for his faults.
                    Analects V (Confucianism)

1243 Knowledge, faith, and right conduct are the true causes of
      final liberation.
                    Sutra-krit-anga (Jainism)

1244 Seek the Lord while he may be found;
      call on him while he is near.
                    Isaiah 55.6 (Judaeo-Christian)

1245 What the gentleman seeks, he seeks within himself;
      what the small man seeks, he seeks in others.
                    Analects XV.21 (Confucianism)

1246 Among the signs of success at the end is the turning to God
      at the beginning.
                    The Book of Wisdom 27 (Sufism)

1247 Make it your ambition to lead a quiet life,
      to mind your own business and to work with your hands.
                    1 Thessalonians 4.11 (Christianity)

1248 The way of life cleaves without cutting
      Which, needless to say,
      Should be man's way.
                    Tao Teh Ching 81 (Taoism)

1249   The practice of self-awakening does not lie in verbal
       arguments.
                   Tan Ching 13 (Zen)

1250   Work out your own salvation with fear and trembling.
                   Philippians 2.12 (Christianity)

1251   Master of his senses and avoiding wrong,
           one should do no harm to any living being,
           neither by thoughts nor words nor acts.
                   Sutra-krit-anga I.11.12 (Jainism)

1252   It is impossible for a man to be saved in ignorance.
                   Doctrine and Covenants 131.6 (Mormonism)

1253   Speak the truth,
           yield not to anger,
           give what you can to him who asks:
           these three steps lead you to the gods.
                   Dhammapada 224 (Buddhism)

1254   When you meet someone better than yourself,
           turn your thoughts to becoming his equal.
                   Analects IV.17 (Confucianism)

1255   He who seeks and uses earnest endeavour finds; and he who
           knocks at the door and is persistent enters.
                   Hadith (Islam)

1256   Nobody hath found God by walking his own way.
                   Adi Granth (Sikhism)

1257   Guard yourself in spirit,
           and do not break faith.
                   Malachi 2.16 (Judaeo-Christian)

1258   Try to realize that you are single and alone,
           thereby you will obtain liberation.
                   Sutra-krit-anga I.10.12 (Jainism)

1259   Let him who seeks continue seeking until he finds.
            Gospel of Thomas II.32.15–16 (Gnosticism)

1260   Vexed is the seeker after this world.
            Rewarded is the seeker after the next world.
        Glad is the seeker after the Lord.
            The Song of the Dervish (Sufism)

1261   Let your aim be one and single;
            Let your hearts be joined in one—
        The mind at rest in unison—
            At peace with all, so may you be.
            Rig Veda X.191.4 (Hinduism)

1262   Seek not what is too difficult for you,
            nor investigate what is beyond your power.
            Ecclesiasticus 3.21 (Judaeo-Christian)

1263   The best that you can seek from Him is that which He seeks
        from you.
            The Book of Wisdom 75 (Sufism)

1264   Give me moral strength and perseverance through good
        purpose!
            Yasna 51.7 (Zoroastrianism)

1265   Doing, knowing, training self,
            Life in utter blamelessness,
        Men are purified by these
            Not by birth and not by wealth.
            Majjhima-Nikaya III.143 (Buddhism)

1266   Ask, and it will be given to you;
            seek, and you will find;
        knock, and the door will be opened to you.
            Matthew 7.7 (Christianity)

1267   Either seek for high position or for God.
            Shaikh Brahm (Sikhism)

1268   According to the purpose which a person has in this world,
       thus does he become on departing hence.
                   Chandogya Upanishad 3.14.1 (Hinduism)

REWARD

1269   As the pains so the gains.
                   Talmud (Judaism)

1270   The life to come holds a richer prize for you than this pres-
       ent life.
                   Koran 93.1 (Islam)

1271   The Lord will reward everyone for whatever good he does.
                   Ephesians 6.8 (Christianity)

1272   Actions receive their reward.
                   Mahavagga 1.38.11 (Buddhism)

1273   Verily, those who believe, and do good works,
           and are steadfast in prayer and give alms:
       for then is their reward with their Lord.
                   Koran 2.277 (Islam)

1274   Let another praise you, and not your own mouth;
           someone else, and not your own lips.
                   Proverbs 27.2 (Judaeo-Christian)

1275   Set thy heart upon thy work, but never on its rewards.
                   Bhagavad Gita 2.47 (Hinduism)

1276   Every soul will be rewarded according to its merit.
                   Koran 3.182 (Islam)

1277   So long as devout zeal is in the heart,
       The reward shall be yours!
                   Yasna 53.7 (Zoroastrianism)

1278   Thou shalt obtain a reward in proportion to what thou hast
       done.
                   Asa Ki War (Sikhism)

1279   Rejoice and be glad,
           because great is your reward in heaven.
                   Matthew 5.12 (Christianity)

1280   He rewards those who earnestly seek Him.
                   Hebrews 11.6 (Christianity)

1281   Give clear appreciation to merit and demerit,
           and deal out to each its sure reward or punishment.
                   Nihongi XXII (Shinto)

1282   According to the labor is the reward.
                   The Sayings of the Fathers 5.26 (Judaism)

1283   Every good deed has its recompense.
                   Shu King 3.3.2.6 (Confucianism)

1284   Whoever seeks the harvest of the world to come,
           to him We will give in great abundance,
           and whoever desires the harvest of this world,
           a share of it shall be his:
           but in the hereafter he shall have no share at all.
                   Koran 42.18 (Islam)

1285   Blinding passions yield bitter fruit.
                   Jatakas 431 (Buddhism)

1286   Restrain your voice from weeping and your eyes from tears,
           for your work will be rewarded.
                   Jeremiah 31.16 (Judaeo-Christian)

1287   When work is done for a reward,
        the work brings pleasure, or pain, or both,
        in its time; but when a man does work in Eternity,
        then Eternity is his reward.
                    Bhagavad Gita 18.12 (Hinduism)

1288   If a misfortune befalls you,
        it is the fruit of your own labors.
                    Koran 42.28 (Islam)

1289   A man can only receive what is given him from heaven.
                    John 3.27 (Christianity)

1290   God does not reward a man for what he does,
        but for what he is.
                    Chuang-tzu (Taoism)

1291   Find the reward of doing right, in right.
                    Bhagavad Gita 2 (Hinduism)

1292   The end does not justify the means.
                    Talmud (Judaism)

SELF

1293   Who sees all beings in his own self,
        and his own self in all beings, loses all fear.
                    Isha Upanishad (Hinduism)

1294   One's own self is difficult to subdue.
                    Dhammapada 159 (Buddhism)

1295   He who conquers others has power of muscles;
        He who conquers himself is strong.
                    Tao Teh Ching 33 (Taoism)

1296   Each creature is born alone; dies also alone;
       alone enjoys his good deeds,
       alone also his bad deeds.
>   Laws of Manu 4.238 (Hinduism)

1297   Behold, the kingdom of God is within you.
>   Luke 17.21 (Christianity)

1298   For thy Self is the master of thyself,
       and thyself is thy refuge.
>   Dhammapada 380 (Buddhism)

1299   Exert and control yourself.
>   Sutra-krit-anga I.2.1.11 (Jainism)

1300   The Self, smaller than small, greater than great,
       is hidden in the heart of that creature.
>   Katha Upanishad 1.2.20 (Hinduism)

1301   Your true self has nowhere to hide;
       When the world is destroyed, it is not destroyed.
>   Mumonkan 33 (Zen)

1302   For what is inside of you is what is outside of you, and the
       one who fashions you on the outside is the one who
       shaped you on the inside.
>   The Thunder, Perfect Mind VI.20.18–23
>   (Gnosticism)

1303   Be free of the bond which encompasses you about,
       And your own self is thereby released.
>   Saraha's Treasury of Songs (Buddhism)

1304   He who knows his own self, knows God.
>   Hadith 282 (Islam)

1305   To know one's self is hard, to know
    Wise effort, effort vain;
    But accurate self-critics are
    Secure in times of strain.
          Panchatantra I (Hinduism)

1306   Difficult to conquer is oneself.
          Uttara-Dhyayana Sutra IX.36 (Jainism)

1307   Cherish that which is within you,
    and shut off that which is without;
    for much knowledge is a curse.
          Chuang-tzu (Taoism)

1308   If spiritual longing be not awakened,
    How can the merits grow within one?
          Mila Grubum (Buddhism)

1309   Knock on yourself as upon a door,
    and walk upon yourself as on a straight road.
          The Teachings
          of Silvanus VII.106.30–33 (Gnosticism)

1310   What I call good at hearing is not hearing others but hearing
oneself.
          Chuang-tzu VIII (Taoism)

1311   The kingdom of heaven is within you;
    and whosoever knoweth himself shall find it.
          New Sayings of Jesus (Christianity)

1312   The truth is spoken; and the self is not obtruded.
          Mahavagga 5.1.28 (Buddhism)

1313   He who knows others is learned;
    He who knows himself is wise.
          Tao Teh Ching 33 (Taoism)

SENSES

1314   The man who wisely controls his senses as a good driver
       controls his horses, and who is free from lower passions
       and pride, is admired even by the gods.
              Dhammapada 94 (Buddhism)

1315   The five colors can blind,
           The five tones deafen,
       The five tastes dull.
              Tao Teh Ching 12 (Taoism)

1316   Know that no sights or sounds can hurt you.
              Tibetan Book of the Dead (Buddhism)

1317   So far are the senses less reliable than the intuitions.
              Chuang-tzu (Taoism)

1318   Thou shalt not let thy senses make a playground of thy
       mind.
              The Voice of the Silence (Buddhism)

1319   Be quick to listen, but take time over your answer.
              Ecclesiastes 5.11 (Judaeo-Christian)

1320   A wise man should strive to restrain his organs which run
       wild among alluring sensual objects, like a charioteer his
       horses.
              Laws of Manu (Hinduism)

1321   The senses of hearing and seeing do not think and are
       obscured by external things.
              Mencius 6 (Confucianism)

1322   Just as the flutterers fall into the lamp,
           So some are bent on what they see and hear.
              Udana (Buddhism)

1323   He that answers before listening—
    that is his folly and shame.
                    Proverbs 18.13 (Judaeo-Christian)

1324   If each man keeps his own sense of sight,
    the world will escape being burned up.
                    Chuang-tzu X (Taoism)

1325   Hearing, seeing, touching, and knowing are not one and
    one; Mountains and rivers should not be viewed in the
    mirror.
                    Hekiganroku 40 (Zen)

1326   To love a thing makes the eye blind, the ear deaf.
                    Talmud (Judaism)

1327   There is nothing more evident than that which cannot be
    seen by the eyes and nothing more palpable than that
    which cannot be perceived by the senses.
                    Doctrine of the Mean 1.3 (Confucianism)

1328   Should he taste savours that are sweet and choice,
    And then again what's bitter to the tongue,
    He should not greedily devour the sweet,
    Nor yet feel loathing for the bitter taste.
                    Samyutta-Nikaya 4.71 (Buddhism)

1329   Ears that hear and eyes that see—
    the Lord has made them both.
                    Proverbs 20.12 (Judaeo-Christian)

1330   For when the mind becomes bound to a passion of the
    wandering senses, this passion carries away man's wis-
    dom, even as the wind drives a vessel on the waves.
                    Bhagavad Gita 2.67 (Hinduism)

1331   Certain colors can be seen; certain colors cannot.
                    Zohar (Kabbalah)

1332 An attentive ear is the desire of the wise.
Ecclesiasticus 3.29 (Judaeo-Christian)

1333 Many a man who sees does not see the Word
And many a man who hears does not hear it.
Rig Veda X.71.4 (Hinduism)

1334 The loss of sight entails forgiveness of sins.
Hadith (Islam)

1335 Though seeing, they do not see;
though hearing, they do not hear or understand.
Matthew 13.13 (Christianity)

1336 If you stick to the eyes, the ears are deafened;
If you discard the ears, the eyes are blinded.
Hekiganroku 56 (Zen)

1337 Let him who has ears hear.
Gospel of Thomas II.44.9–10 (Gnosticism)

1338 Mastery over the senses is brought about through concentrated meditation upon their nature, peculiar attributes, egoism, pervasiveness, and useful purpose.
Yoga Sutras of Patanjali (Hinduism)

SERVICE

1339 To live to benefit mankind is the first step.
The Voice of the Silence (Buddhism)

1340 Make the foot firm of those who have stumbled and stretch out your hands to those who are ill.
The Gospel of Truth I.33.1–3 (Gnosticism)

1341 The purpose of the magnanimous is to be found in procuring benefits for the world and eliminating its calamities.

Sun Yi-jang (Confucianism)

1342 If you do not tend one another,
who is there who will tend you?

Vinaya-Pitaka 1.302 (Buddhism)

1343 Those that love not live only for themselves: as to those they love, they will give their very bones for helping others.

Tirukkural (Hinduism)

1344 There is no physician like experience.

Hadith 190 (Islam)

1345 The gentleman is easy to serve but difficult to please;
the small man is difficult to serve but easy to please.

Analects XIII.25 (Confucianism)

1346 Serve the Lord your God.

Exodus 23.25 (Judaeo-Christian)

1347 A sensible man does not devise resources:
The greater his use to others
The greater their use to him,
The more he yields to others
The more they yield to him.

Tao Teh Ching 81 (Taoism)

1348 One satisfies the debt to his fellow men by doing good to them.

Mahabharata 12.293.10 (Hinduism)

1349 It is better to serve others than to make others serve you.

The Sentences of Sextus XII.29.17–19
(Gnosticism)

1350   Where all things prosper, you can find the use.
Hekiganroku 47 (Zen)

1351   Who receives unto himself the calmuny of the world
Is preserver of the state.
Tao Teh Ching 78 (Taoism)

1352   Ruin not thyself with scant service.
Asa Ki War (Sikhism)

1353   Carry each other's burdens.
Galatians 6.2 (Christianity)

1354   Thinking to serve his kinsfolk, one must need know man.
Doctrine of the Mean 20.7 (Confucianism)

1355   Let your thoughts be fixed upon that which will rehabilitate
the fortunes of mankind and sanctify the hearts and souls
of men.
Gleanings from the
Writings of Baha'u'llah XLIII (Baha'i)

1356   Afford help to the helpless.
Avesta (Zoroastrianism)

1357   We should remember the poor.
Galatians 2.10 (Christianity)

1358   In life we should be of use to others.
Li Ki 2.1.3.22 (Confucianism)

SIN

1359   Think not of the faults of others,
of what they have done or not done.
Think rather of your own sins,
of the things you have done or not done.
Dhammapada 50 (Buddhism)

1360   There is no death without sin.
Talmud (Judaism)

1361   Those who perform meditation for even one session
Destroy innumerable accumulated sins.
Song of Meditation (Zen)

1362   All have sinned and fall short of the glory of God.
Romans 3.23 (Christianity)

1363   Fight thine own sins, not the sins of others.
Analects XII.21 (Confucianism)

1364   If any one of you is without sin,
let him be the first to throw a stone.
John 8.7 (Christianity)

1365   When confessed the sin becomes less, since it becomes
truth.
Satapatha Brahmana (Hinduism)

1366   Commit a sin twice and it will not seem to thee a crime.
Talmud (Judaism)

1367   There are three ways of committing sins: by our own actions, by authorizing others; and by approval.
Sutra-krit-anga I.1.2.26 (Jainism)

1368   Anyone then, who knows the good he ought to do and
doesn't do it, sins.
James 4.17 (Christianity)

1369   He that commits sin commits it against his own soul.
Koran 4.111 (Islam)

1370 Do not be so confident of atonement that you add sin to sin.
Ecclesiasticus 5.5 (Judaeo-Christian)

1371 The essence of sin is excess and deficiency;
whereas the essence of virtue is the mean.
Dinkard VI.X.11 (Zoroastrianism)

1372 Be sure that your sin will find you out.
Numbers 32.23 (Judaeo-Christian)

1373 Sin is the slime that adheres to our bodies,
minds like the frogs which no bloom can attract.
Adi Granth (Sikhism)

1374 The wages of sin is death.
Romans 6.3 (Christianity)

1375 Good deeds make amends for sins.
Koran 11.110 (Islam)

1376 All your sins are truly without number.
The Book of Enoch 62.12 (Judaism)

1377 To commit no sin is better than retribution and renunciation of sin.
Dadistan-i-Dinik XLI.11 (Zoroastrianism)

1378 Your sin prompts your mouth;
you adopt the tongue of the crafty.
Job 15.5 (Judaeo-Christian)

1379 He who recognizes that he sins and does not cease from sinning is called a foolish man.
Sutra-krit-anga II.2.78 (Jainism)

1380 Envy not the glory of a sinner:
for you know not what shall be his end.
Ecclesiasticus 9.11 (Judaeo-Christian)

1381   Roam the world and see what was the end of the guilty.
Koran 27.66 (Islam)

1382   In all you do, remember the end of your life,
and then you will never sin.
Ecclesiasticus 7.36 (Judaeo-Christian)

1383   Sin neither openly nor in secret.
Koran 6.119 (Islam)

1384   The day of atonement is the day which never ends.
Talmud (Judaism)

SOUL

1385   The soul is not a man, or a woman,
nor what is neither a woman nor a man.
Svetasvatara Upanishad V (Hinduism)

1386   A beneficent soul will be abundantly gratified.
Talmud (Judaism)

1387   Let every soul look to what it offers for the morrow.
Koran 59.18 (Islam)

1388   The soul is without shape, taste, tangibility, smell, or col-
our; it consists of knowledge which in one moment knows
the whole universe; it has supreme felicity, being free from
attachment, aversion, desires and passions; it is also im-
perishable and pure.
Paramatma-prakasha (Jainism)

1389   The soul who sins is the one who will die.
Ezekiel 18.20 (Judaeo-Christian)

1390   He has gained nothing who has not gained the soul.
Fragments of the Nasks (Zoroastrianism)

1391   Woe to the flesh that depends on the soul;
woe to the soul that depends on the flesh.
Gospel of Thomas II.51.10–12 (Gnosticism)

1392   All that is exists for the sake of the soul.
Yoga Sutras of Patanjali (Hinduism)

1393   What shall a man give in exchange for his soul?
Matthew 16.26 (Christianity)

1394   In times which test the soul,
Lose yourself in revelry.
Divan (Sufism)

1395   The soul-breath directs and trains the human being and in-
itiates him into every straight path.
Zohar (Kabbalah)

1396   For every soul there is a guardian watching over it.
Koran 86.1 (Islam)

1397   He who wins the soul is wise.
Proverbs 11.30 (Judaeo-Christian)

1398   At the end of life the soul goes forth alone.
Fo-Sho-Hing-Tsan-King 1560 (Buddhism)

1399   In immortality shall the soul of the righteous be joyful; its
perpetuity shall be the torments of the liars.
Yasna 45.7 (Zoroastrianism)

1400   The human soul is, in its essence, one of the signs of God,
a mystery among His mysteries.
Gleanings from the
Writings of Baha'u'llah LXXXII (Baha'i)

1401   In your patience possess ye your souls.
Luke 21.19 (Christianity)

1402   Just as the ocean is full of brilliant, pure waters, so is this powerful soul known as the compendium of knowledge.
Samaveda II.3.5 (Hinduism)

1403   Wretched is the body that is dependent upon a body, and wretched is the soul that is dependent on these two.
Gospel of Thomas II.48.4–7 (Gnosticism)

1404   A vast, deep and childlike faith in all, a universal clemency, and a close veiling of his own god-like inherent virtues, are the traits which mark a noble soul.
Garuda Purana (Hinduism)

1405   All else is false and unsteady but that light—that light lit in your soul.
Dasam Granth (Sikhism)

1406   No soul shall bear another's burden.
Koran 35.18 (Islam)

1407   The soul of a man is his friend when by the Spirit he has conquered his soul; but when a man is not lord of his soul then this becomes his own enemy.
Bhagavad Gita 6.6 (Hinduism)

SUFFERING

1408   Your suffering is due to your own bad karma, nothing more.
Tibetan Book of the Dead (Buddhism)

1409   One suffers most who is most selfish.
Tao Teh Ching 13 (Taoism)

1410   If you should suffer for what is right, you are blessed.
           1 Peter 3.14 (Christianity)

1411   One should not be mindful of suffering in his own life and
           unmindful of suffering in the lives of others.
           Gorikai (Shinto)

1412   Not made by self is this puppet
           Nor is this misfortune made by others.
           Conditioned by cause it comes to be,
           By breaking of cause it is stopped.
           Samyutta-Nikaya 1.134 (Buddhism)

1413   Sufferings atone more than sacrifice.
           Talmud (Judaism)

1414   There is forgiveness in proportion to the deficiency which
           the body has suffered.
           Hadith (Islam)

1415   Where there is affection there is misery.
           Garuda Purana (Hinduism)

1416   The wise man should consider that not he alone suffers; all
           creatures in the world suffer.
           Sutra-krit-anga I.2.1.13 (Jainism)

1417   Blessed is the man who has suffered and found life.
           The Gospel of Thomas II.43.7–9 (Gnosticism)

1418   No suffering befalls the man who calls nothing his own.
           Dhammapada 221 (Buddhism)

1419   In order that your sadness over anything be little,
           let your joy over it be little.
           The Book of Wisdom 226 (Sufism)

1420   He who has suffered in his body is done with sin.
           1 Peter 4.1 (Christianity)

1421 For neither the kingdom of the earth, nor the kingdom of the gods in heaven, could give me peace from the fire of sorrow which thus burns my life.
> Bhagavad Gita 2.8 (Hinduism)

1422 Bring not suffering upon yourself by indulgence in selfishness.
> Gorikai (Shinto)

1423 It is better, if it is in God's will,
to suffer for doing good than for doing evil.
> 1 Peter 3.17 (Christianity)

1424 How should grief affect him who looks upon pain and pleasure as the same.
> Adi Granth (Sikhism)

1425 If ever for man were it possible to fold the tent of the sky, in that day he might be able to end his sorrow without the help of God.
> Svetasvatara Upanishad (Hinduism)

1426 Learn how to suffer and you shall be able not to suffer.
> Acts of John (Christianity)

THOUGHT

1427 Thought is act in fancy.
> Bhagavad Gita 3 (Hinduism)

1428 Know that things arise from your own thoughts.
> Tibetan Book of the Dead (Buddhism)

1429 Do not think of yourself more highly than you ought, but rather think of yourself with sober judgment.
> Romans 12.3 (Christianity)

1430   Thinking good and evil is attachment to heaven and hell.
        Mumonkan (Zen)

1431   If your thought is a rose, you are a rose garden,
        and if it is a thorn, you are fuel for the furnace.
        Masnavi 113 (Sufism)

1432   Think good thoughts with thy mind.
        Avesta (Zoroastrianism)

1433   Before a step is taken, the goal is reached;
        Before the tongue is moved, the speech is finished.
        Mumonkan 48 (Zen)

1434   To hope for miraculous blessings, and still have weary
        opinions—that prolongs the bondage.
        Bya Chos (Buddhism)

1435   If you start to doubt then doubt has no end.
        Gorikai (Shinto)

1436   The external universe is created by our thoughts,
        as also the imaginary world.
        Hathayoga Pradipika (Hinduism)

1437   Do not think of the past;
        always think of the future.
        Tan Ching 20 (Zen)

1438   The Lord knows the thoughts of man;
        he knows they are futile.
        Psalms 94.11 (Judaeo-Christian)

1439   He who gives no thought to difficulties in the future is sure
        to be beset by worries much closer at hand.
        Analects XV.12 (Confucianism)

1440   If thought be distracted we lie in the fangs of the passions.
        Bodhicaryavatara (Buddhism)

1441 Worthy ends do not come about from wishing.
Hitopadesa (Hinduism)

1442 All your lives meditate on God.
Adi Granth (Sikhism)

1443 He who has reached the state of thought is silent.
Lieh Tzu 4 (Taoism)

1444 Just as space, essentially indiscriminate, reaches everywhere,
just so the immaculate Element which in its essential
nature is Thought, is present in all.
Ratnagotravibhaga IX.49 (Buddhism)

1445 As one thinks, so one becomes.
Ashtavakra Gita (Hinduism)

1446 Why may the thought be sin to-day that yesterday was pure.
Gulshan-i-raz (Sufism)

TRUTH

1447 He who knows the truth is not equal to him who loves it.
Analects VI.18 (Confucianism)

1448 You will know the truth,
and the truth will set you free.
John 8.32 (Christianity)

1449 A man who recognizes the truth delights in nothing else.
Acharanga Sutra I.2.6.5 (Jainism)

1450 When a man speaks words of truth he speaks words of
greatness: know the nature of truth.
Chandogya Upanishad (Hinduism)

1451   He is true in the truest sense of the world who is true in
      word, in thought, and in deed.
          Hadith 401 (Islam)

1452   Love truth and peace.
          Zechariah 8.19 (Judaeo-Christian)

1453   Speak the truth, though harsh it be:
      Blarney is true enmity.
          Panchatantra I (Hinduism)

1454   Birds flock with their kind; so truth returns to those who
      practice it.
          Ecclesiasticus 27.9 (Judaeo-Christian)

1455   Prove constant to truth.
          Acharanga Sutra I.3.2.1 (Jainism)

1456   Truth all religion comprehends, in truth alone is justice
      placed, in truth the words of God are based.
          Ramayana 2.14 (Hinduism)

1457   Man is known as true when truth is in his heart.
          Asa Ki War (Sikhism)

1458   Blame not before you have examined the truth.
          Ecclesiasticus 11.7 (Judaeo-Christian)

1459   If you want the truth to stand clear before you, never be for
      or against it.
          On Trust in the Heart (Zen)

1460   Swear not by God except it to be the truth.
          Hadith (Islam)

1461   Everything depends on truth.
          Adi Granth (Sikhism)

1462   He who sees that the Lord of all is ever the same in all that
is, immortal in the field of mortality – he sees the truth.
Bhagavad Gita 13.27 (Hinduism)

1463   Truth is heavy, therefore few care to carry it.
Talmud (Judaism)

1464   Whoso hath seen me hath seen the truth.
Gulshan-i-raz (Sufism)

1465   We cannot do anything against the truth,
but only for the truth.
2 Corinthians 13.8 (Christianity)

1466   Knowing the truth, one should live up to it.
Sutra-krit-anga I.2.3.15 (Jainism)

1467   Those who imagine truth in untruth, and see untruth in
truth, never arrive at truth but follow vain desires.
Dhammapada 11 (Buddhism)

1468   It is a faithful person fond of learning who is the worker of
the truth.
The Sentences of Sextus XII.33.26–27
(Gnosticism)

1469   The name of God is our merchandise,
Truth is the trade we pursue.
Adi Granth (Sikhism)

1470   One truthful man is better than the whole world speaking
falsehood.
Sad Dar 62.5 (Zoroastrianism)

1471   I have no greater joy than to hear that my children are walking in the truth.
3 John 4 (Christianity)

1472   Of a truth there is no such thing as sickness.
Kojiki (Shinto)

1473   Knowing truth, your heart will ache no more with error.
Bhagavad Gita 4 (Hinduism)

1474   Truth is knowledge of things as they are,
and as they were, and as they are to come.
Doctrine and Covenants 93.24 (Mormonism)

1475   The man who loves truth is better than the man who knows
it, and the man who finds happiness in it is better than
the man who loves it.
Analects V (Confucianism)

1476   Truth is my capital, Truth is my trade,
and the produce I store is in my heart.
Adi Granth (Sikhism)

1477   To know the Truth is to see the oneness of the Self with
God.
Bhagavata Purana (Hinduism)

1478   There is no need to seek Truth, only stop having views.
On Trust in the Heart (Zen)

1479   The lip of truth will be established forever,
but the tongue of falsehood only till I wink my eye.
Zohar (Kabbalah)

1480   Truth obtains victory, not untruth.
Mundaka Upanishad 3.1.6 (Hinduism)

1481   Know that the Truth is sacred regardless of its source,
despite its seeming vagueness or incredibility.
Tibetan Book of the Dead (Buddhism)

UNITY

1482 All are the same, none is separate;
a single form, a single creation.
Dasam Granth (Sikhism)

1483 The earth is but one country, and mankind its citizens.
Gleanings from the
Writings of Baha'u'llah CXIV (Baha'i)

1484 When male and female combine,
all things achieve harmony.
Tao Teh Ching 42 (Taoism)

1485 One Lord, one faith, one baptism.
Ephesians 4.5 (Christianity)

1486 For him who sees everywhere oneness,
how can there be delusion or grief?
Isha Upanishad (Hinduism)

1487 When even one particle stirs,
the whole universe is involved;
a blossom opens and the world responds.
Hekiganroku 19 (Zen)

1488 All things are already complete in us.
Mencius 7 (Confucianism)

1489 Light and darkness, life and death, right and left, are
brothers of one another.
Gospel of Phillip II.53.14–16
(Gnosticism)

1490 When there is no distinction between Body, Speech, and
Mind, then the true nature of the Innate shines forth.
Saraha's Treasury of Songs (Buddhism)

1491 He that planteth and he that watereth are one.
1 Corinthians 3.8 (Christianity)

1492 Those who love pleasure and power hear and follow their
      words: they have not the determination ever to be one
      with the One.
                    Bhagavad Gita 2.44 (Hinduism)

1493 Everything that is a complex event
      Proceeds by way of causes and conditions,
      And the events mutually cause and condition each other.
                    Lalitavistara XIII.99 (Buddhism)

1494 Whoever believes that the All itself is deficient is himself
      completely deficient.
                    Gospel of Thomas II.46.19–20 (Gnosticism)

1495 Who sees the many and not the One wanders on from death
      to death.
                    Katha Upanishad (Hinduism)

1496 One in All
         All in One—
      If only this is realized,
         No more worry about your not being perfect.
                    On Trust in the Heart (Zen)

1497 Because there is one loaf, we, who are many, are one body,
      for we all partake of the one loaf.
                    1 Corinthians 10.17 (Christianity)

1498 Knowing one thing, I know all;
         Knowing all, I know that they are one.
                    Mila Grubum (Buddhism)

1499 Pursue not the outer entanglements,
         Dwell not in the inner void
      Be serene in the oneness of things
         And [dualism] vanishes by itself.
                    Shijin-no-Mei (Zen)

1500   He who sees all beings in the Self,
  and the Self in all beings, hates none.
    Isha Upanishad (Hinduism)

1501   There is one body, and one Spirit.
    Ephesians 4.4 (Christianity)

1502   He is a just man who regards all parts from the point of view
  of the whole.
    Chuang-tzu XXV (Taoism)

1503   Do not discriminate, but see things as one.
    Saraha's Treasury of Songs 26 (Buddhism)

1504   God is one.
    Galatians 3.20 (Christianity)

VIRTUE

1505   He indeed is rich who is rich in virtues.
    Bhagavata Purana (Hinduism)

1506   Virtue never stands alone.
    Analects IV.25 (Confucianism)

1507   Virtuous men regard pleasures as equal to diseases.
    Sutra-krit-anga I.2.3.2 (Jainism)

1508   If virtue perishes, charity perishes.
    Tao Teh Ching 38 (Taoism)

1509   Proclaim your virtues in a whisper,
  and your faults in a loud voice.
    Talmud (Judaism)

1510   Virtue means realization in one's self of what is good.
Li Ki 17.1.8 (Confucianism)

1511   Courtesy is the lord of all the virtues.
Gleanings from the
Writings of Baha'u'llah (Baha'i)

1512   Human life is lost without virtue.
Adi Granth 78 (Sikhism)

1513   Virtue is the root: wealth is the result.
The Great Learning (Confucianism)

1514   The virtuous man is happy in this world.
And he is happy in the next.
Dhammapada 18 (Buddhism)

1515   The man who does not display his virtue is truly virtuous.
Tao Teh Ching 38 (Taoism)

1516   Virtue held in rememberance is a kind of immortality.
The Wisdom of Solomon 4.1 (Judaeo-Christian)

1517   As riches adorn a house, so virtue adorns the person.
Li Ki 39.6 (Confucianism)

1518   Be not afraid of virtues.
Iti-vuttaka 22 (Buddhism)

1519   They who have no virtue, insist on their rights.
Tao Teh Ching 79 (Taoism)

1520   Through riches and the highest pleasures my soul has the
reward for its virtues.
Uttara-Dhyayana Sutra XIII.10 (Jainism)

1521   As muddied garments dirty
    All that you sit upon,
So, when one virtue tumbles,
    The rest are quickly gone.
              Panchatantra IV (Hinduism)

1522   To prize the effort above the prize, that is virtue.
              Analects VI (Confucianism)

1523   True modesty is the source of all virtues.
              Hadith 302 (Islam)

1524   Be virtuous, but without being consciously so.
              Chuang-tzu (Taoism)

1525   Virtue is spotlessness of mind; all else is mere noise.
              Tirukkural (Hinduism)

1526   Virtue, which is of all existences the greatest, the best, the finest, never parts from a man.
              Avesta (Zoroastrianism)

1527   Perfect virtue acquires nothing;
    therefore it obtains everything.
              Tao Teh Ching 38 (Taoism)

WEALTH

1528   All wealth is obtained by the love of God.
              Adi Granth (Sikhism)

1529   Do not wear yourself to get rich;
    have the wisdom to show restraint.
              Proverbs 23.4 (Judaeo-Christian)

1530   Content is the greatest wealth.
              Dhammapada 204 (Buddhism)

1531   Money causes pain in getting;
     In the keeping, pain and fretting;
     Pain in loss and pain in spending:
     Damn the trouble never ending.
         Panchatantra I (Hinduism)

1532   If you have money, do not lend it at interest,
     but give it to one from whom you will not get it back.
         Gospel of Thomas II.48.36; 49.1–2 (Gnosticism)

1533   Who is rich? He who is satisfied with his lot.
         The Sayings of the Fathers 4.1 (Judaism)

1534   Man cannot be satisfied with wealth.
         Katha Upanishad I.27 (Hinduism)

1535   Lazy hands make a man poor,
     but diligent hands bring wealth.
         Proverbs 10.4 (Judaeo-Christian)

1536   There is nothing to be proud of in money.
         The Sayings of Sri Ramakrishna (Hinduism)

1537   He who has riches is far above him who has none.
         Avesta (Zoroastrianism)

1538   Better a little with righteousness than much gain with injustice.
         Proverbs 16.8 (Judaeo-Christian)

1539   No one hath brought wealth with him;
     and no one shall take it away.
         Kabir's Sloks (Sikhism)

1540   With right and wrong eliminated,
     gains and losses are forgotten.
         Hekiganroku 84 (Zen)

1541   You cannot serve both God and money.
> Matthew 6.24 (Christianity)

1542   Wealth and rank attained through immoral means have as
much to do with me as passing clouds.
> Analects VII.16 (Confucianism)

1543   Those who make wealth their all in all cannot bear loss of
money.
> Chuang-tzu XIV (Taoism)

1544   Wealth is good if sin has not tainted it.
> Ecclesiastes 13.24 (Judaeo-Christian)

1545   The greatest wealth consisteth in being charitable.
> Subhashita Ratna Nidhi (Buddhism)

1546   He who loves gold will not be justified,
and he who pursues money will be led astray by it.
> Ecclesiasticus 31.5 (Judaeo-Christian)

1547   What avail riches for the practice of religion?
> Uttara-Dhyayana Sutra XIV.17 (Jainism)

WISDOM

1548   Wisdom is proved right by her actions.
> Matthew 11.19 (Christianity)

1549   Wisdom is a stray, and wherever the believer finds it,
he is most rightfully entitled to it.
> Hadith (Islam)

1550   In this world, few are born with knowledge:
wisdom is the produce of earnest meditation.
> Nihongi XXII (Shinto)

1551 The wisdom of a learned man comes by opportunity of leisure.
> Ecclesiasticus 38.24 (Judaeo-Christian)

1552 One can come to be a wise man by hearing a great deal and following the good, and by seeing a great deal and remembering it.
> Analects I (Confucianism)

1553 O fool, the body of a gnat enshrines wisdom.
> Gulshan-i-raz (Sufism)

1554 Wisdom is better than strength.
> Ecclesiastes 9.16 (Judaeo-Christian)

1555 Make wisdom thy mother.
> Adi Granth (Sikhism)

1556 He who is awakened amongst men preaches the unparalleled wisdom.
> Acharanga Sutra I.6.1.1 (Jainism)

1557 Pursue wisdom like a hunter,
and lie in wait on her paths.
> Ecclesiasticus 14.22 (Judaeo-Christian)

1558 If any of you lack wisdom,
let him ask of God.
> James 1.5 (Christianity)

1559 Silence is the fence of wisdom.
> The Sayings of the Fathers 3.17 (Judaism)

1560 Great wisdom is generous;
petty wisdom is contentious.
> Chuang-tzu (Taoism)

1561 Do not forsake wisdom, and she will protect you;
love her, and she will watch over you.
Proverbs 4.6 (Judaeo-Christian)

1562 A merely striking beauty
Is not so hard to find;
A rarer gem is wisdom,
Far-reaching power of mind.
Panchatantra I (Hinduism)

1563 He who created wisdom is wiser than his works.
The Odes of Solomon 7 (Christianity)

1564 It is blowing through a bamboo to teach wisdom to the dull.
Adi Granth (Sikhism)

1565 The price of wisdom is beyond rubies.
Job 28.19 (Judaeo-Christian)

1566 Meditation itself is the substance of wisdom;
wisdom itself is the function of meditation.
Tan Ching 13 (Zen)

1567 Wisdom will not enter a shifty soul,
nor make her home in a body that is mortgaged to sin.
The Wisdom of Solomon 1.4 (Judaeo-Christian)

1568 This is the quintessence of wisdom;
not to kill anything.
Sutra-krit-anga (Jainism)

1569 Great men are not always wise.
Job 32.9 (Judaeo-Christian)

1570 By my praise of Perfect Wisdom
All the merit I may rear,
Let that make the world devoted
To this wisdom without peer.
Diamond Sutra 142.21 (Buddhism)

1571   Better is the man who hides his folly than the man who
hides his wisdom.
Ecclesiasticus 20.31 (Judaeo-Christian)

1572   In what can wisdom not prevail?
Panchatantra I (Hinduism)

1573   Let the wise man shew forth his wisdom,
not in words, but in good works.
The First Epistle of Clement
to the Corinthians 17.36 (Christianity)

1574   Ignorance creates Rest and Unrest;
Wisdom neither loves nor hates.
On Trust in the Heart (Zen)

1575   Wisdom preserves the life of its possessor.
Ecclesiastes 7.12 (Judaeo-Christian)

1576   Wisdom is better than the wealth of every kind which is in
the world.
Menog-i-Khrad 47.6 (Zoroastrianism)

1577   There are levels upon levels within the mystery of a dream,
all within the mystery of wisdom.
Zohar (Kabbalah)

1578   Wine and music gladden the heart,
but the love of wisdom is better than both.
Ecclesiasticus 40.20 (Judaeo-Christian)

1579   Those who themselves have seen the Truth can be thy
teachers of wisdom.
Bhagavad Gita 4.24 (Hinduism)

1580   The true beginning of wisdom is the desire to learn.
The Wisdom of Solomon 6.17 (Judaeo-Christian)

1581 Better than the best of riches is wisdom
—for once won, none may lose her again.
Hitopadesa (Hinduism)

WORK

1582 When a man does the work God gives him,
no sin can touch this man.
Bhagavad Gita 18.47 (Hinduism)

1583 Joyful is the accumulation of good work.
Dhammapada 118 (Buddhism)

1584 Honest work bears glorious fruit.
*The Wisdom of Solomon 3.15
(Judaeo-Christian)*

1585 Strive to excel each other in good works.
Koran 5.53 (Islam)

1586 The good work of a man who hath relinquished a bad habit
and through his good capabilities engageth in renunciation of sin, advanceth unto the future existence.
Shayast-na-shayast IX.6 (Zoroastrianism)

1587 When work is done as sacred work, unselfishly, with a
peaceful mind, without lust or hate, with no desire for
reward, then the work is pure.
Bhagavad Gita 18.23 (Hinduism)

1588 Where the labour is great, the gain is the more.
*Epistle of Ignatius
to Polycarp 1.6 (Christianity)*

1589 To attack a task from the wrong end can do nothing but harm.

   Analects II.16 (Confucianism)

1590 In all my learning, tasks, and duties,
   May I master them quickly and effectively.

   Tibetan Book of the Dead (Buddhism)

1591 Be a lover of work and a hater of lordship:
   and do not cater to the ruling powers.

   The Sayings of the Fathers 1.10 (Judaism)

1592 Do thy duty, even if it be humble,
   rather than another's, even if it be great.

   Bhagavad Gita 3.35 (Hinduism)

1593 We are laborers together with God.

   1 Corinthians 3.9 (Christianity)

1594 A workman who wants to do his work well must first prepare his tools.

   Analects XV (Confucianism)

1595 The sleep of a laboring man is sweet.

   Ecclesiastes 5.12 (Judaeo-Christian)

1596 All men in due time must suffer the fruit of their works.

   Sutra-krit-anga I.2.1.6 (Jainism)

1597 Give the laborer his wages before his perspiration is dry.

   Hadith 266 (Islam)

1598 Love thy work.

   Talmud (Judaism)

1599 How shalt thou be saved without good works.

   Adi Granth (Sikhism)

1600 All hard work brings a profit,
  but mere talk leads to poverty.
  Proverbs 14.23 (Judaeo-Christian)

1601 A man attains perfection when his work is worship of God,
  from which all things come and who is in all.
  Bhagavad Gita 18.46 (Hinduism)

WORLD

1602 The life of this world is but a sport and a pastime.
  Koran 6.32 (Islam)

1603 Nothing is more admirable than to sever,
  were it only for a time, all earthly relations.
  Oracle of Hachiman (Shinto)

1604 If any man love the world,
  the love of the father is not in him.
  1 John 2.15 (Christianity)

1605 When a man considers this world as a bubble of froth, and
  as the illusion of an appearance, then the king of death
  has no power over him.
  Dhammapada 170 (Buddhism)

1606 Do not maintain that the world is an illusion;
  maintain that it exists.
  Sutra-krit-anga II.5.13 (Jainism)

1607 This world is a prison for the Faithful,
  but a Paradise for unbelievers.
  Hadith 434 (Islam)

1608 The world is preserved by three things:
            truth, justice, and peace.
                        The Sayings of the Fathers 1.18 (Judaism)

1609 In all the world there is no such thing as a stranger.
                        Munetada (Shinto)

1610 Take not the world for your lord;
            lest it take you for its slave.
                        Logia (Christianity)

1611 The world is a man, and man is a world.
                        Gulshan-i-raz (Sufism)

1612 What good will it be for a man if he gains the whole world,
            yet forfeits his soul?
                        Matthew 16.26 (Christianity)

1613 The world is boundless and eternal;
            it exists for eternity and shall not perish.
                        Sutra-krit-anga I.1.4.6 (Jainism)

1614 This world is a world of work, the next, a world of recompense.
                        Talmud (Judaism)

1615 Delight not yourselves in the things of the world and its
            vain ornaments, neither set your hopes on them.
                        Gleanings from the
                        Writings of Baha'u'llah CXVI (Baha'i)

1616 He who has recognized the world has found the body,
            but he who has found the body is superior to the world.
                        Gospel of Thomas II.47.12–14 (Gnosticism)

1617 The world is all made out of one clay,
            but the potter fashions it into vessels of many sorts.
                        Adi Granth (Sikhism)

1618   Be in this world like a traveler.
Hadith 438 (Islam)

1619   The world and its desires pass away.
1 John 2.17 (Christianity)

1620   The world is bent on pleasure.
Dhammampada 217 (Buddhism)

1621   The best book is the world.
Talmud (Judaism)

1622   The world is lost to those who try and win it.
Tao Teh Ching 48 (Taoism)

1623   If the whole world and all treasures were yours, you would still not be satisfied.
Uttara-Dhyayana Sutra XIV.39 (Jainism)

1624   The world will be what you make of it.
Munetada (Shinto)

WORSHIP

1625   It is not possible for you to know God when you do not worship him.
The Sentences of Sextus XII.32.12–14 (Gnosticism)

1626   Any object of adoration is better than self-worship.
Divan (Sufism)

1627   Every man should follow his own religion.
The Sayings of Sri Ramakrishna (Hinduism)

1628   Love the Lord your God with all your heart and with all
your soul and with all your strength and with all your
mind.
Luke 10.27 (Christianity)

1629   Not to follow after fools, but to follow after the wise: The
worship of the worshipful—this is the greatest blessing.
Sutta-Nipata 259 (Buddhism)

1630   The highest religion of man is unselfish love of God.
Bhagavata Purana (Hinduism)

1631   Worship the Lord your God, and serve him only.
Matthew 4.10 (Christianity)

1632   Make the practice of religion your board and truth your
pieces.
Adi Granth (Sikhism)

1633   Worship, above all, is truthfulness.
Satapatha Brahmana 2.2.2.20 (Hinduism)

1634   Always and in everything let there be reverence.
Li Ki 1.1.1.1 (Confucianism)

1635   Forsaking all else, worship only him.
Adi Granth (Sikhism)

1636   Every religion is nothing but one of such paths that lead to
God.
The Sayings of Sri Ramakrishna (Hinduism)

1637   Worship is the outward expression of wisdom,
and the Lord himself inspires it.
Ecclesiastes 15.10 (Judaeo-Christian)

1638   As all rivers must go to the ocean, so all acts of worship
reach him as the ultimate goal.
Mahanirvana Tantra (Buddhism)

1639   Looking upon all beings as myself, in thought, word, and deed is the best of all methods of worship.
Srimad Bhagavatam 11.29.19 (Hinduism)

1640   God is spirit, and his worshippers must worship in spirit and in truth.
John 4.24 (Christianity)

1641   Thank him by whose gifts thou liveth.
Asa Ki War 22 (Sikhism)

1642   Even those who in faith worship other gods,
because of their love they worship me,
although not in the right way.
Bhagavad Gita 9.23 (Hinduism)

1643   Not in any religion have men's eyes been awry,
not in any sect have their thoughts been perverse.
Adi Granth (Sikhism)

1644   Different creeds are but different paths to reach the Almighty.
The Sayings of Sri Ramakrishna (Hinduism)

1645   Do not decry other sects, do not depreciate others, but rather honour whatever in them is worthy of honour.
Asoka's Edicts (Buddhism)

1646   The kinds of flowers vary, yet all worship is one.
Vemana's Padyamulu (Hinduism)

Sources

Acharanga Sutra — Jain text of Mahavira's teachings compiled by Bhadrabahu, an Indian sage, at the beginning of the third century B.C. A discourse on rules and teachings, its name is derived from the word *achara* (conduct).

Acts — Christian text said to have been written by St. Luke in A.D. 62. It examines the theme of Jesus's continuing ministry through the Holy Spirit and discusses the history of Christianity up to Paul's arrival in Rome.

Acts of John — Christian text written by Leucius Charinus, author of other Apocryphal books, in the second or third century A.D. Part of the Apocryphal New Testament, it has an ascetic hostility towards marriage and sex.

Adi Granth — Sikh text compiled in 1603–1604 by Arjan, the fifth Sikh Guru. Containing the sayings of the principal Sikh Gurus, it means "first book," distinguishing it from later Sikh texts.

Aitareya Brahmana — Hindu text written by an unknown author sometime in the seventh century B.C. It consists of three short sections examining the Hindu notions of creation and the self.

Alma — Mormon text said to have been written by Alma and compiled by Joseph Smith, Jr., in 1830. It details the history of the Nephites, a people who Mormons believe lived in North America, between 91 and 52 B.C.

Amos — Judaeo-Christian text written by Joel, the son of Petheul, ca. 830 B.C. It discusses the coming of "the Day of the Lord," encouraging the reader to find the proper attitude and life in the eyes of the Lord.

The Analects (Lun Yu) — Confucian text compiled by Mencius (372–289 B.C.), a follower of Confucius. One of the Four Books of the Confucian canon, it is a collection of Confucius's sayings regarded as the prime example of Confucian writing.

Anguttara-Nikaya — Buddhist text of the Buddha's teachings committed to writing by an unknown author during the third or second century B.C. It examines the doctrines of Buddhist life.

Anugita — Hindu text written by an unknown author during the third or second century B.C. Part XIV of the Mahabharata, it praises the Brahmin (priest) caste; however, it is considered by some to be a dishonest and insipid imitation of the Bhagavad Gita.

Asa Ki War — Sikh text written by an unknown author during the early eighteenth century. Part of the Panjgranthi prayer book, it is a collection of hymns of praise to God traditionally sung or chanted every morning by Sikh minstrels.

Ashtavakra Gita — Hindu text written by an unknown author before the second century B.C. It is a dialogue between the sage Ashtavakra and King Jakana discussing the renunciation of material objects and the quest for knowledge and liberation.

Asoka's Edicts — Buddhist text written by Asoka (270–232 B.C.), an Indian king. It is a collection of Buddhist maxims that Asoka ordered carved on rocks to promote the concept of *dhamma* (law) throughout India after a terrible war had cost him nearly half a million casualties.

The Awakening of Faith — Buddhist text written by Asvaghosha, an Indian sage, in the first century A.D. It examines the Buddhist concept of salvation by faith alone.

Atharva Veda — Hindu text compiled by unknown authors at the beginning of the second millennium B.C. It is a compendium of primitive Indian hymns, rituals, chants, and observations of daily life.

Avesta — Zoroastrian text said to have been written by Zoroaster (626–551 B.C.), although the date may be as early as 2000 B.C. Once written in gold ink on twelve thousand ox hides, it was destroyed by Alexander the Great in 330 B.C., of which only the liturgy of the text has survived.

Avesyaka Sutra — Jain text written by an unknown author in the second or first century B.C. It is a collection of teachings and sayings from other Jain sutras such as the Prakirnaka, and is considered canonical only by the Sthanakavasi sect.

Bani — Hindu text written by Dadu (1544–1603), an Indian sage, during the sixteenth century. It contains hymns on topics such as truth and faith that have been set to music by some Hindus.

Bhagavad Gita — Hindu text written by an unknown author ca. A.D. 200. Part of the Mahabharata, it is the best known and most important Hindu text, consisting of a discourse between the warrior prince Arjuna and Krishna, a Hindu god disguised as Arjuna's charioteer. Discussing the three paths of salvation for the Hindu (jhana, karma, and bhakti), its name means "Song of the Lord."

Bhagavata Purana — Hindu text written during the tenth century A.D. by an unknown author in Tamil. It studies the life and teachings of Vishnu as well as examining the teachings of the Vedas, the Upanishads, and the concept of bhakti.

Bharavi's Kiratarjuniya — Hindu text said to have been written by Bharavi, an Indian sage, in the sixth century A.D. It is a poem on social conduct that describes man and his relationship with nature.

Bodhicaryavatara — Buddhist text written by Santideva, an Indian teacher, during the seventh century A.D. It is a poem that praises the life of the Buddhist who through self-sacrifice attains wisdom and enlightenment.

The Book of Certitude (Kitab-I-Iquan) — Baha'i text written by Baha'-u'llah between 1856 and 1863 while in Baghdad. It is a collection of essays examining Baha'i beliefs regarding God and the world.

The Book of Enoch — Hebrew text written by numerous authors during the first millennium B.C. Considered inspired until the third century A.D.; it is a collection of various commentaries on the Messiah, sin, and judgment.

The Book of Faith and Reliance — Kabbalah text written by Jacob ben Sheset, a rabbi from Gerona, in the thirteenth century. It is esoteric in nature, studying the interdependence of faith and reliance.

The Book of Filial Piety (Hsiao King) — Confucian text compiled by Confucius during his lifetime (551–478 B.C.). It discusses religious ritual, domestic life, and filial piety.

The Book of Thomas the Contender — Gnostic text recorded by Mathaias (possibly another name for St. Matthew) during the first half of the third century A.D. It is a conversation between the resurrected Jesus and Judas Thomas, his alleged brother.

Book of Wisdom (Kitah al-Hikam) — Sufi text written by Ibn 'Ata'illah, a Sufi saint, in 1288. Written before the death of his master, Shaykh Abu'l-'Abbas al-Mursi, it is a collection of proverbial sayings regarding the pursuit of a proper life.

Brihad-Aranyaka Upanishad — Hindu text written by an unknown author ca. 500 B.C. It is the oldest Upanishad, discussing the origin of life, the soul, and life after death.

Buddha-Karita — Buddhist text written by Asvaghosha, the twelfth Buddhist patriarch, ca. A.D. 70. It examines the life and the doctrine of the Buddha, and was translated from Sanskrit into Chinese by Dharmaraksha in A.D. 420.

Bya Chos — Buddhist text written by an unknown lama of the Kahgyutpa sect during the eighteenth century. It is a poem attempting to explain the moral doctrines of the Buddha in an allegorical setting among birds.

Chandogya Upanishad — Hindu text written by an unknown author ca. 500 B.C. Considered to be the second oldest Upanishad, it is devoted to the instruction of worship and meditation.

Chou-ilueh-li — Taoist text written by Chou Kung (Duke of Chou), a Chinese statesman, before his death in 1105 B.C. It was originally written as a code of rules for state officials during the Chou Dynasty.

Chuang-tzu — Taoist text based on the wisdom of Chuang-tzu, compiled by his followers during the fourth and early third centuries B.C. It is a collection of stories examining Taoist principles.

Chucho-Jijitsu — Shinto text written by Yamaga Soko in 1669 while he was exiled in Akoo. It discusses mythological stories of Shinto theology and ritual as well as imperial tradition.

Colossians — Christian text written by the apostle Paul ca. A.D. 61–63 during his imprisonment in Rome. It is a refutation of the heresies and false teachings in which the people of Colosse were engaged.

1 Corinthians — Christian text written by the apostle Paul in A.D. 55. It is a letter to the citizens of Corinth, a city located in Greece, written to give them practical advice regarding Christian conduct.

2 Corinthians — Christian text written by the apostle Paul in A.D. 57. He wrote this letter to defend his motives and authority in writing the first letter to the citizens of Corinth.

Dadistan-i-dinik — Zoroastrian text written in the ninth and tenth century by Zoroastrian followers in Iran. It is a series of ninety-two questions and answers containing Zoroastrian teachings lost since the destruction of the Avesta by Alexander the Great's troops.

Dasam Granth — Sikh text written by Gobind Singh, the tenth Sikh Guru, in 1708. It is a collection of hymns and poetry that discusses the Sikh beliefs and tenets laid down by Guru Nanak in the Adi Granth.

Dasaveyaliya — Jain text written by Svayambhava, the fifth Patriarch of the Jain church, during the fourth century B.C. It is a discussion of the essential Jain doctrines proposed by Mahavira.

Deuteronomy — Judaeo-Christian text said to have been written by Moses as a farewell address to the Israelites between 1580 and 1280 B.C. It is one of the most often quoted books by Jesus and his Apostles, with over eighty references in the New Testament.

Dhammapada — Buddhist text of the Buddha's sayings compiled ca. 300 B.C. It is perhaps the most accessible Buddhist text in terms of availability and teaching.

Dharmapada — Buddhist text compiled by an unknown author before the third century B.C. Written in Sanskrit, it differs slightly from the Dhammapada, which was written in Pali.

The Dialogue of the Saviour — Gnostic text written by an unknown author sometime during the first three centuries A.D. It records a conversation between Jesus and his disciples.

Diamond Sutra (Vajracchedika) — Buddhist text written by an unknown author during the early third century B.C. Known as the "Perfection of Wisdom" teaching, it is a metaphysical dialogue between Buddha and his disciples.

Digha Nikaya — Buddhist text of the Buddha's teachings compiled by an unknown author at the beginning of the first century A.D. It is a collection of long discourses by the Buddha on various subjects.

Dinkard — Zoroastrian text written in the ninth and tenth century by Zoroastrian followers in Iran. It contains ancient Zoroastrian teachings, traditions, and customs paraphrased from lost portions of the Avesta.

Divan — Sufi text written by Hafiz (1320–1390), a Persian poet, during the fourteenth century. It is a collection of poetry and mystic songs of flight and love, thematically unifying man and God.

Doctrine and Covenants — Mormon text written by Joseph Smith, Jr., before his death in 1844. The book is considered to be the revealed word of God regarding aspects of both a temporal and spiritual nature.

Doctrine of the Mean (Chung-Yung) — Confucian text written in the fourth century B.C. by K'ung Chi, a grandson of Confucius. One of the Four Books of Confucianism, it examines the social values of Confucian philosophy, as well as the Confucian idea of the two states of fundamental mind: the pre-stirred, where the mind is in an innocent state; and the post-stirred, where the mind has come into contact with the events of the world.

Ecclesiastes — Judaeo-Christian text said to have been written by King Solomon in the fourth or third century B.C.; however, an unknown author is now believed to have used Solomon as a literary medium to convey his message. It chastises man for looking at other philosophies other than the Way of God to satisfy his pleasuresome appetites.

Ecclesiasticus — Judaeo-Christian text written by Jesus, the son of Sirach, ca. 180 B.C. It is a collection of wise sayings and parables, much like its Old Testament counterpart, Proverbs.

Ephesians — Christian text written by St. Paul in A.D. 62. It examines the Christian analogy of the Church as a body with Christ as the head, as well as asking Christians to lead their lives as if they were Jesus's disciples.

Epistle of Ignatius to Polycarp — Christian text written by Ignatius during the first century A.D. It is a letter to Polycarp, a disciple of the apostle John, regarding the Christian way of life.

Epistle of Ignatius to the Ephesians — Christian text written by Ignatius, a Christian missionary, during the first century A.D. It is a letter to the Ephesians urging them to accept Jesus as their savior.

Epistle of Ignatius to the Philadelphians — Christian text written by Ignatius during the first century A.D. It was written to the citizens of Philadelphia, a city in Asia Minor, urging them to adopt Christianity.

Epistle to the Son of the Wolf — Baha'i text written by Baha'u'llah while in Baghdad between 1856 and 1863. It discusses the concept of a universal God and acceptance of all faiths.

Exodus — Judaeo-Christian text said to have been written by Moses between 1580 and 1280 B.C. It examines the theme of the redemption of the Israelites as a chosen people.

Ezekiel — Judaeo-Christian text written by Ezekiel during the sixth century B.C. It relates the Babylonian exile, and discusses the restoration of the Israelites from exile to spiritual renewal.

The First Epistle of Clement to the Corinthians — Christian text written by Clement, a disciple of Peter and future Bishop of Rome, between A.D. 150 and 215. It is a letter to the city of Corinth that draws an analogy between Jesus's resurrection and the rising of the mythical phoenix from its own ashes.

The Forty-two Traditions of An-Nawawi — Islamic text written by An-Nawawi (1233–1278), an Islamic sage. It studies the tenets of Islam for the Moslem in a changing world.

Fo-Sho-Hing-Tsan-King — Buddhist text written in Dharmaraksha, an

Indian priest, in A.D. 420. Translated from the Buddha-Karita of Asvaghosha, it differs slightly from the Sanskrit original.

Fragments of the Nasks — Zoroastrian text compiled between the third and fourth centuries A.D. by Zoroastrian followers living in Iran. It is a fragment of the original twenty-one *nosks* (acts of worship) or chapters of the Avesta.

Galatians — Christian text written by the apostle Paul in A.D. 53. It was composed as a response to Jewish Christians who insisted that obeying certain Mosaic laws were necessary to attain salvation.

Garuda Purana — Hindu text written before the fifth century A.D. by an unknown author. Named for the garuda, a bird of Hindu mythology that was half-man and half-vulture, it is a manual used by Smarta priests.

Genesis — Judaeo-Christian text said to have been written by Moses between 1580 and 1280 B.C. Containing the Creation Myth, it discusses the early history of the Israelites as well as defining law, sin and righteousness for Jews.

Gleanings from the Writings of Baha'u'llah — Baha'i text written by Baha'u'llah during his exile in Bagdad from 1856 to 1863. It examines the Baha'i concept of the universality of all religions.

Gobind Singh — Sikh text containing the teachings of Gobind Singh (1666–1708), the Tenth Guru of the Sikhs, compiled by his followers after his death in the early part of the eighteenth century. It stresses that the Adi Granth is the continuation of the Sikh nation in lieu of future Gurus.

Gorikai — Shinto text compiled by the followers of Kawate Bunjiro (1814–1883), a Shinto priest. It examines Bunjiro's teachings of direct communion with God and a dual consciousness.

Gospel of Phillip — Gnostic text written by an unknown author from Syria during the middle of the third century A.D. It contains ethical statements pertaining to the Gnostic view of life.

Gospel of Thomas — Gnostic text written by Didymos Judas Thomas, believed by members of the Syrian Church to have been the twin brother of Jesus, ca. A.D. 150. It is a collection of sayings, proverbs, parables, and prophecies of Jesus that parallels parts of Matthew, Mark, and Luke.

Gospel of Truth — Gnostic text said to have been written by Valentinius in the middle of the second century A.D. It is a meditation studying the person and the work of Jesus.

The Great Learning — Confucian text written by an unknown author in the first century B.C. It is a commentary on a short selection of Confucius's writings.

Gulshan i-Raz — Sufi text written by Sa'du'd-Din Mahmud Shabistari, a famous mystic of Tabriz, at the beginning of the fourteenth century. It discusses the Sufi concepts of the incomprehensible Divine Will, and the oneness of God and the world.

Habakkuk — Judaeo-Christian text written by Habakkuk, a prophet and contemporary of Jeremiah, during the seventh century B.C. It is a dialogue between Habakkuk and God, emphasizing the importance of faith over knowledge.

Hadith — Islamic text compiled by the followers of Mohammed after his death in A.D. 632. It is a compilation of the traditional sayings of Mohammed.

Haggai — Judaeo-Christian text written by Haggai in 520 B.C. It examines the Christian concepts of obediance, prosperity, and piety.

Hathayoga Pradipka — Hindu text written by Swatmaram Swami during the nineteenth century. It discusses the concept of *hatha* (force) in yoga, occultist in nature, with claims made of levitation and surviving a live burial.

Hazrat Ali — Sufi text written by Hazrat Ali, a companion and son-in-law of Mohammed as well as the fourth Caliph of Islam, during the seventh century A.D. It is a collection of letters and sermons on various aspects of life such as philosophy, religion, law, and politics.

Hebrews — Christian text written by an uncertain author (Paul, Barnabas, Luke, Timothy, and Phillip among others have been considered) ca. A.D. 68. It stresses the superiority of Jesus to demonstrate what the author believed to be the inferiority of Judaism.

Hekiganroku — Zen text compiled by Cho-mei-en, a Zen monk, ca. A.D. 1300. Reconstructed from the koans of Setcho (980–1052) and the commentary on thte koans by Engo (1063–1135), it examines Zen theory in the perception and understanding of the world.

Helaman — Mormon text said to have been written by Helaman and his sons, compiled in 1830 by Joseph Smith. It is an account of the Nephites, a group believed by Mormons to have settled in North America, between 52 and 1 B.C.

Hitopadesa — Hindu text said to have been written by Visnu Sarman, a teacher of the sons of King Sundarsana, but more likely attributed to Narayana, a Bengali Tantric writer of the third century A.D. It is a collection of fables and sayings that helps the Hindu in his daily activities.

Hymns of Guru Nanak — Sikh text written by Guru Nanak (1479–1539), the first Sikh Guru. It is a collection of poetry-like prose and vernacular hymns on the theme of *bhakti*, or devotion.

I Ching — Taoist text said to have been written by Futtsi, a Chinese sage, in the third millennium B.C. Perhaps the oldest book in existence, it has been used for 5000 years as a divining tool to predict the future.

Intimate Conversations (Munajat) — Sufi text written by Khwaja 'Abdullah Ansari before his death in 1089. It is a dialogue between the author and God on Sufi doctrines.

Isaac of Ninevah — Christian text written during the sixth century A.D. by Isaac, a Syrian recluse. It is an examination into the life of exiled Jews living in Ninevah.

Isaiah – Judaeo-Christian text written by Isaiah, a Hebrew prophet, ca. 690 B.C. It is an omen to the pagan kings of Jerusalem warning them of their eventual destruction. It is reputed that King Manasseh executed the prophet for writing it by sawing him in two.

Isha Upanishad – Hindu text written by an unknown author ca. 500 B.C. It discusses the existence of a monistic God for Hindus.

Itu-vuttaka – Buddhist text written by an unknown author in the latter part of the first century B.C. It is a compilation of the teachings and thoughts of the Buddha.

James – Christian text written by James, the Lord's brother, ca. A.D. 150. It urges the world to embrace the teachings of Jesus, and to exercise faith in their everyday lives.

Japji Granth – Sikh text written by Guru Nanak (1469–1539) in the sixteenth century. It is the morning prayer of the Sikhs, praising God and his love.

Jatakas – Buddhist text compiled by Buddhaghosa in the fifth century A.D. A collection of 547 birth-stories of the Buddha, it reflects teachings through the previous existence of the Buddha in animal forms such as a lion, a bird, and an elephant.

Jeremiah – Judaeo-Christian text written by Baruch, a scribe of the priest Jeremiah, during the early part of the sixth century B.C. It is a compilation of the prophecies of Jeremiah, relating his attempt to call his people back to God before the Babylonian exile.

Job – Judaeo-Christian text written by an unknown author before 200 B.C. It discusses Job's questioning of his faith in God after several tragedies occur, bringing him great suffering.

John – Christian text written by St. John ca. A.D. 90. Possibly Gnostic in origin and development, it describes the life of Jesus according to St. John in a more poetic and craftful manner than the other Gospels.

1 John – Christian text written by St. John between A.D. 85–95. Written as a tract against the heretical Gnostic teachings, it reminds Christians of their coming salvation.

3 John – Christian text written by St. John between A.D. 85–95. It was written as a text supporting the early Christian teachers.

Judges – Judaeo-Christian text written by Samuel, King of the Israelites, ca. 1000 B.C. It characterizes the life of Israel, where God is present in all that happens.

Kabir's Sloks – Sikh text written by Kabir (1440–1518), a mystic poet, during the fifteenth century. Read by Hindus, Sufis, and Moslems, it presents a universal God who is the same for everyone, regardless of religious or ethnic belief.

Katha Upanishad – Hindu text written by an unknown author ca. 500 B.C. It studies the Hindu concept of the indestructible soul, and is also quoted in the Bhagavad Gita.

Kaushitaki Upanishad – Hindu text written between 500 and 400 B.C. by an unknown author. It examines Hindu teachings pertaining to the exploration of the Self.

Kirtan Sohila — Sikh text compiled in 1603–1604 by Arjan, the fifth Guru. It is a prayer that is recited before retiring each evening.

Knowledge of Spirit (Atma Bodha) — Hindu text written by Sankaracharya, a philosopher and religious organizer, in the ninth century A.D. It attempts to bring a reconciliation of the various Hindu sects back to the teachings of the Vedas.

Kojiki — Shinto text written in A.D. 712 by O-No-Yasumaro from the teachings of the sage Hieda no Are upon the request of Jito, the Emperor's widow. Literally meaning "Records of Ancient Matters," it contains myths and stories pertaining to Japan's ancient history.

Koran — Islamic text of revelations given to Mohammed by Allah, compiled by Zeid ibn Thabit, Mohammed's adopted son, after his death in A.D. 632. It is a collection of teachings arranged from the longest to the shortest, making frequent references to Old Testament figures such as Adam, Abraham, Noah, Joseph, and Moses.

Lalitavistara — Buddhist text written by an unknown author in the fifth century A.D. It is a biography of the Buddha important to Mahayanists because it does not deify the Buddha as other biographies do.

Lankavatara Sutra — Buddhist text written by Asanga in the fourth century A.D. Part of the "thought-school" system, it teaches that nothing but thought is important, as well as embracing that the human soul is God. It is also accepted by Zen followers.

Laws of Manu — Hindu text said to have been written by Manu before the flood, but refined by Hindu lawmakers during the first millennium B.C. It is a collection of myths and laws pertaining to all aspects of man's existence on earth.

Leviticus — Judaeo-Christian text said to have been written by Moses ca. 1450 B.C. It discusses the regulations given by God to the Israelites, epitomized by the concepts of atonement, holiness, and sacrifice.

Li Ki — Confucian text compiled and written by Confucius's disciples after his death in 479 B.C. It is a collection of historical information and ceremonial regulations.

Lieh Tzu — Taoist text said to have been written by Lieh Tzu in the fourth century B.C., although the author was probably a creation of the Chinese sage Chuang-tzu. It presents the Taoist creation theory in a bizarre tone of humor.

Logia — Christian text written by an unknown author between A.D. 150 and 300. It was created from a group of sayings attributed to Jesus that were found in Upper Egypt, the Greek Bible, and the Tischendorf Bible.

Lotus Sutra (Saddharmapundarika) — Buddhist text compiled by an unknown author during the first or second century A.D. It is a religious drama examining the manifestations of the Buddha said to have been given from the Buddha's death bed.

Luke—Christian text written by St. Luke before A.D. 62. The oldest Gospel upon which Matthew and Mark are based, it presents the most complete account of the life of Jesus, including a description of his birth not found in the other Gospels.

Mahabharata—Hindu text said to have been written by the great Indian sage Vyasa, but probably written by a number of authors. The longest poem in the world (totalling over one hundred thousand verses), it is thought to have been compiled in three separate sections: (1) a series of popular poems collected between the sixth and fourth century B.C.; (2) sectarian poems written during the second century B.C.; and (3) an encyclopedia of theology, philosophy, politics, and law, written between the first and second century A.D.

Mahanirvana Tantra—Hindu text written by Ram Mohan (1772–1833) during the eighteenth century. It is an exposition of the worship of the Supreme Brahman, expounding on the areas of conduct, worship, and family rite.

Mahavagga—Buddhist text written by an unknown author before the third century B.C. Meaning "great section," is is a collection of treatises, narratives, ballads, and biographies of the Buddha.

Maitri Upanishad—Hindu text written by an unknown author ca. 500 B.C. It examines teachings that supposedly strengthen and enlighten the mind.

Majjhima-Nikaya—Buddhist text compiled by Sariputta, a follower of Buddha, before 200 B.C. One of the four Nikayas, it is a collection of medium length discourses and dialogues attributed to the Buddha.

Malachi—Judaeo-Christian text written by Malachi in 433 B.C. It is a treatise on the sovereignty of God and the rebuilding of Israel; it is called an "oracle" by its author.

The Manual of Discipline—Hebrew text written by an unknown author betwen 100 and 75 B.C. It is a compilation of the codes and principles that the Qumran brotherhood used in their religious practice.

Mark—Christian text written by St. Mark between A.D. 67–70. It is important for its portrayal of Jesus as the Divine Son, the Son of God.

Markandeya Purana—Hindu text written by an unknown author in the fourth century A.D. It discusses the legends of the ancient Hindu gods, expressing the concept of *ragas,* or passion.

Masnavi—Sufi text written by Jalalu 'D-Din Rumi (1207–1273), a Persian poet of the thirteenth century. It is a poem examining the concept of unity of Being (*wahdat al-wujud*), or the oneness of the universe.

Matthew—Christian text written by St. Matthew before A.D. 70. Written as an introduction to Christianity, it studies the life and teachings of Jesus. It also attempted to convince the Jews that Jesus was their Messiah.

Mencius—Confucian text written by Mencius (372–289 B.C.), a Chinese sage and follower of Confucius. One of the Four Books of Confucianism, it is a discussion of social, psychological, economic, and political issues.

Menog-i Khrad—Zoroastrian text written at the beginning of the third century A.D. by Zoroastrian followers in Iran. It is compiled from an ancient Zoroastrian book of revelation.

Mila Grubum—Buddhist text written by Milarepa (1052–1135), a Buddhist monk, during the twelfth century A.D. It is a series of dialogues between Milarepa and his followers.

Milindapanha—Buddhist text written by King Milinda (Menander), a Greek ruler of the Punjab area, between 155–100 B.C. It discusses issues such as karma, faith, meditation, individuality, and the soul.

Mishkat-el-Masabih—Islamic text written by an unknown author during the fourteenth century A.D. It is a collection of sayings attributed to Mohammed; commentary was added by Shaikh Abdul Hag Muhaddith during the seventeenth century.

Moroni—Mormon text said to have been written by Moroni, a Mormon prophet, compiled in 1830 by Joseph Smith. It details the history, beliefs and lives of the Nephites, a people believed to have resided in North America in the centuries before and after Jesus.

Mumonkan—Zen text written by Mumon Ekai, a Zen monk, in 1228. It is a collection of forty-eight koans describing the world.

Mundaka Upanishad—Hindu text written by an unknown author between 500 and 300 B.C. It describes a personal theism, and also is found as an attachment to the Atharva Veda.

Munetada—Shinto text written by Munetada, a Japanese poet of the nineteenth century. It is a poem examining Munetada's concept of the ultimate combination of *kami* and the Divine life.

Namhardi Rahit-nama—Sikh text written by Satguru Ram Singh, the twelfth Sikh Guru, in the eighteenth century. It is a composition of the Namhardi Sikhs that asks all Sikhs to give equal importance to the Adi Granth and the Dasam Granth.

Narada Smriti—Hindu text written by Narada, an Indian teacher, before the seventh century A.D. It is a commentary on the older Vedas, containing religious and legal teachings.

New Sayings of Jesus—Christian text compiled by an unknown author in the first century A.D. following Jesus's death. It is a collection of sayings and teachings attributed to Jesus.

Nihongi—Shinto text written by Futo-no-Yasumaro and Prince Toneri of Japan in A.D. 720. Literally meaning "The Chronicles of Japan," it examines the ancient history of the Japanese.

Nirgrantha-Pravachana—Jain text written by an unknown author during the latter part of the fourteenth century. It is a sermon discussing the proper attitude and conduct for Jain life as seen by the Nirgranthas, a sect of Jains who follow Mahavira in their practice of naked asceticism.

Numbers—Judaeo-Christian text written by Moses between 1450 and 1410 B.C. It reflects the ancient laws and regulations of the Israelites during their exodus in the wilderness.

The Ocean of Delight for the Wise (Lodam-Gawai-Roltso) — Buddhist text written by an unknown Tibetan monk during the eighth and ninth centuries A.D. It offers advice on human character and actions.

The Odes of Solomon — Christian text compiled by an unknown author during the first century A.D. It has been claimed by Jewish, Christian, and Gnostic scholars; nevertheless, it is thought to have been the first Christian hymn book.

On the Origin of the World — Gnostic text written by an unknown author from Alexandria at the beginning of the fourth century A.D. It offers a Gnostic explanation of the world's creation.

On Trust in the Heart — Zen text written by Seng-ts'an, the third Patriarch of the Dhyana sect, before his death in A.D. 606. It is an exposition of traditional Mahayana doctrines.

Oracle of Hachiman — Shinto shrine and inscription created between A.D. 860–880 by the followers of Hachiman, the Shinto war god. An important deity, Hachiman was a powerful protector of human life, a god of agriculture, and a guardian deity giving peace and happiness to Japan.

Oracle of Tatsuta — Shinto inscription from the *ginja* (shrine) established before A.D. 1000 in Nara prefecture. The temple is dedicated to Tatsuta, a deity responsible for protecting the health of people as well as promoting the harvest of abundant crops.

Oracle of the Deity Atsuta — Shinto temple and inscriptions established at the end of the first century A.D. in the Aichi prefecture. The primary deity of the shrine is the "Grass-moving sword" (Kusanagi-no-Tsurugi), a sword of an ancient prince that is still at the shrine.

An Oracle of the Deity Temmangu — Shinto temple created by an unknown group at the Kitano Shrine in Heian-kyo, Japan, sometime during the beginning of the tenth century A.D. It discusses the teachings of the spirit Temmangu, a deity worshiped for literature and learning.

Oracle of the Gods of Kasuga — Shinto temple containing inscriptions of the religion, established in A.D. 859 at Kasuga. The temple worships various gods such as Takemika-dzuchi, a father god; and Futsunushi, a master.

Panchatantra — Hindu text said to have been written by Vishnusharma, a Brahmin priest, during the second century B.C. It is a collection of animal fables that uses human faults for the benefit of teaching the wise conduct of life (*niti*).

Pand Nameh — Zoroastrian text written by Adarbad Marespend in A.D. 330. Part of the Khorda Avesta (Small Avesta), it is an Iranian commentary on the larger Avesta.

Paramatma-prakasha — Jain text written by Sri-Yogindra Akalanka before the tenth century A.D. One of Akalanka's "Examinations," it opposes theistic teaching, arguing instead for the divine spirit of the human soul.

1 Peter—Christian text written by the apostle Simon Peter in A.D. 64. It is a commentary on the proper ideals for Christian life and duties.

2 Peter—Christian text written by the apostle Simon Peter in A.D. 66. It warns Christians about false teachers, and nominates virtue as the best defense against heresy.

Philippians—Christian text written by the apostle Paul between A.D. 54–62. It is a letter composed for the people of Philippi while Paul was incarcerated in Rome, urging them to correct certain aspects of their church.

Pravacana-sara—Jain text written by Kunda Kunda in the first century B.C. It is an outline of the "right doctrine" for the Jain to follow.

Proverbs—Judaeo-Christian text written by King Solomon (although certain sections were composed anonymously) and edited down to its final form ca. 400 B.C. It is a collection of ethical and moral teachings stressing the aspects of good, evil, and wisdom.

Psalms—Judaeo-Christian text said to have been written by David, although compiled during both pre–Exilic and post–Exilic dates (1050–520 B.C.). It is divided into five sections (Genesis, Exodus, Leviticus, Numbers, and Deuteronomy) comprising a wonderful answer to Israel's role as God's chosen people, and is famous for its beautiful poetry, some of which has been set to music.

Ramayana—Hindu text written by Valmiki, an Indian sage, between the sixth and fourth centuries B.C. It is a collection of poems and theistic essays describing the life of Prince Rama, a legendary Hindu figure, while introducing the essential Hindu concept of *bhakti* (devotion).

Ratnagotravibhaga—Buddhist text written by Saramati, an Indian sage, during the sixth century A.D. It is a Mahayana Buddhist shastra discussing the Three Jewels of Buddhism: Buddha, Doctrine, and Community.

Rig Veda—Hindu text composed between 2000 and 1600 B.C. by unknown authors. One of the four primary Vedas, it is a collection of 1028 hymns praising the gods of India; its reading and teaching is confined to the higher castes of Indian society.

Rokeach—Hebrew text written by an unknown Jewish author during the Middle Ages. Named after someone who prepares medicine out of plants, it examines Jewish mysticism.

Romans—Christian text written by the apostle Paul ca. A.D. 55–56. Composed for a group of Christians in Rome, it discusses the highlights of Jesus's life and teachings as well as establishing a broad doctrine of Christianity.

Sad Dar—Zoroastrian text composed by Zoroastrians who escaped the destruction of Persia by the Greeks in the fourth century B.C. Compiled from lost portions of the Avesta, it contains comments and interpretations on the text.

Saikondan—Taoist text written by an unknown author at an uncertain date. It is mentioned in Sessan Amakuki's On Hakuin's Zazen Wasan, a discourse on Zen meditation.

Samadhi Shataka — Jain text written by Pujyapada Devadin, an Indian sage, in the latter half of the fifth century A.D. It is a collection of one hundred sayings of profound contemplation, reflecting on the sight or display of all forms.

Samaveda — Hindu text written by an unknown author between 1200 and 1000 B.C. Used as a chant while drinking *soma* (a ritual juice), it is fairly repetitive of the Rig Veda, with only 78 different verses.

1 Samuel — Judaeo-Christian text written by Samuel, a king of Israel, up to his death and completed by Abiathar, a compatriate of Samuel, ca. 1000 B.C. It discusses the theme of God as the Divine Ruler in man's life as well as relating the history of the Israelites from the time of the judges to the monarchy of Saul.

Samyutta-Nikaya — Buddhist text written by an unknown author during the second or third century B.C. One of the four Nikayas, it is composed of dialogues arranged by subject and includes the first sermon by the Buddha after he attained enlightenment.

Saraha's Treasury of Songs (Dohakosha) — Buddhist text written by Saraha, a Buddhist saint, sometime between the second and sixth centuries A.D. It is a collection of proverbial quotations reflecting the Buddhist way of life.

Sarva-Darsana-Samgraha — Hindu text written by Madhava, an Indian sage, in 1380. It is a treatise of Hindu skepticism, containing teachings that dispute the precepts of the orthodox school.

Satapancasatkastotra — Buddhist text written by Matraceta, an Indian teacher, ca. A.D. 100. It is a series of verses describing the Buddha with fervent adoration.

Satapatha Brahmana — Hindu text said to have been written by Yajnavalkya in the seventh century B.C. It urges Hindus to study not only the Vedas, but also texts such as the Upanishads and other works of Hindu mythology.

The Sayings of Sri Ramakrishna — Hindu text written by Sri Ramakrishna (1834–1886), a modern Hindu saint, during the nineteenth century. It reflects the duplicity of religions and their various paths to God.

The Sayings of the Fathers — Hebrew text written by various authors during the first millennium A.D. It is a brief compendium of maxims found in the Mishnah, a Hebrew text of new laws based on interpretations of the older laws located in the Talmud.

The Second Apocalypse of James — Gnostic text written by an unknown author in the first or second century A.D. It contains secret teachings and revelations of Jesus to James, the Lord's brother.

Selections from the Writings of 'Abdu'l Baha — Baha'i text written by 'Abdu'l Baha (Abbas Effendi, 1843–1921, the eldest son and spiritual successor of Baha'u'llah). It describes the concept of a universal God.

The Sentences of Sextus — Gnostic text written by an unknown author in the first or second century A.D. It is a compendium of adages and aphorisms of wisdom, and strongly stresses the restraint of the passions.

Shaikh Brahm—Sikh text written by Shaikh Brahm, a Sikh sage, in the seventeenth or eighteenth century. It is a collection of poems and teachings that examines the Sikh way of life.

Shayast-na-shayast—Zoroastrian text written at the beginning of the third century A.D. by Zoroastrian followers in Iran. It contains teachings and interpretations of an ancient Zoroastrian book of rituals lost since the destruction of the Avesta by Alexander the Great's troops.

Shih King—Confucian text written by an unknown author between 1766 and 566 B.C. It is a collection of poems, hymns and ballads, not all of which are religious in nature.

Shijin-no-mei—Zen text written by Seng-ts'an, the third Patriarch in the Dhyana school of Chinese Buddhism, before his death in 606 A.D. It discusses the Zen concept of the absolute Mind.

Shrichakrasambhara Tantra (Sri-Cakra-Samvara)—Buddhist text written by an unknown Tibetan monk during the eighth or ninth century A.D. It is a Tibetan Tantra examining esoteric doctrines from an expository point of view.

Shu King—Confucian text edited and prefaced by Confucius in the sixth or fifth century B.C. It is a collection of dialogues spoken by characters who recall the history of China from 2357 to 627 B.C.

Siri-siri-valaka—Jain text written by an unknown author at an uncertain date. It is a treatise on Jain conduct and living.

Sloks of Shaikh Farid—Sikh text compiled by an unknown author during the early sixteenth century from the teachings of Farid, a Sikh sage. It offers the commentary of Farid on the instructions of the Sikh texts and Gurus.

Sohar Rahiras—Sikh text written in 1603–1604 by Arjan, the fifth Guru. It is a prayer that is recited in the evening by Sikh minstrels and followers.

Song of Enlightenment—Zen text written by Yoka Daishi before his death in A.D. 713. It is a Zen commentary on the mind, enlightenment, and social conduct.

Song of Meditation—Zen text written in the eighteenth century by Hakuin, considered to be the father of modern Zen. It is an attempt to define Zen concepts in simple everyday terms.

Song of Solomon—Judaeo-Christian text written by King Solomon during the tenth century B.C. It is a poem of love; the object of love has been speculated as God, the Messiah, mankind, and a woman.

Song of the Dervish—Sufi text written by Khwaja 'Abdullah Ansari before his death in A.D. 1089. Part of the Munajat, it is a short collection of wisdom, aphorisms, and adages.

Songs of Kabir—Sikh text written by Kabir (1440–1518), a mystic poet, during the fifteenth century. Read by Hindus, Sufis, and Sikhs as well, it is a collection of poetry that presents a synthetic God who is the same for everyone, regardless of religious or ethnic belief.

Srimad Bhagavatam — Hindu text written by an unknown author in the third century B.C. It examines the life and teachings of Sri Krishna, and is considered to be one of the primary texts of Hinduism.

The Staff of Wisdom (Prajna-Danda) — Buddhist text written by Nagarjuna, the first great philosophical systemizer of Mahayana doctrines, during the second century A.D. It discusses Buddhist theories on the nature of ultimate reality.

Subhashita Ratna Nidhi — Buddhist text written by Saskya Pandita, the Grand Lama of Saskya, during the thirteenth century. Meaning "wellsaid" or "bravo," it is a praise for proper actions, character, and conduct.

Sukhmani — Sikh text written by Guru Arjan in the late sixteenth or early seventeenth century. It is a poem included by many Sikhs in their morning prayers of devotion.

Sun Yi-jang — Confucian text written by Motse, a Chinese sage, during the fifth or fourth century B.C. It outlines a system of worship that contradicts normal Confucian teachings, and was subsequently frowned upon by the followers of Confucius.

The Supreme Teaching — Hindu text written by an unknown author ca. 500 B.C. Included in the Upanishads, it addresses the topics of liberation, karma, and death.

Sutra-krit-anga — Jain text written at the beginning of the third century B.C. by Bhadrabahu, an Indian sage. Written to instruct Jain monks, it contains the essence of Jain teachings.

Sutta-Nipata — Buddhist text written by an unknown author in the latter half of the first millennium B.C. Considered to be the oldest of the Buddhist scriptures, it discusses the Buddha's renunciation of the physical world.

Svetasvatara Upanishad — Hindu text written ca. 500 B.C. by Svetasvatara, a Hindu teacher. It examines the Hindu concepts of *bhakti, maya,* and *yoga,* as well as presenting the union of Atman and Brahman.

T'ai Shang Kan Ying P'ien — Taoist text written by an unknown author sometime during the eleventh century A.D. It is an examination of actions and their consequences, whether they be good or bad.

Taittiriya Upanishad — Hindu text written by an unknown author ca. 500 B.C. It discusses the monistic concept of Brahman, the primary Hindu God.

Talmud — Hebrew text of civil and canonical law written by over two thousand teachers during its twelve centuries of existence. Consisting of the Mishnah (teachings) and the Gemara (the discussion on the teachings), it is an interpretation of Hebrew law.

Tan Ching — Zen text written by Hui-neng (Yeno), the sixth Zen patriarch, before his death in A.D. 712. It studies the perception of the physical world and its seemingly simple structure.

Tao Teh Ching—Taoist text said to have been written by Lao-tzu (604–531 B.C.), an ancient Chinese sage. It examines the mystical concept of Tao as well as various social and nature issues.

Tattvartha Sutra—Jain text written by Amritachandra, an Indian sage, at the beginning of the tenth century A.D. It discusses the teachings that Jains believe help them to reach perfection.

The Teachings of Silvanus—Gnostic text written by Silvanus, a possible companion of Paul, in the late second or early third century A.D. It studies the theme of universal salvation, regardless of religion, due to the Divine element that is inherently innate.

1 Thessalonians—Christian text written by the apostle Paul in A.D. 50. It is a letter composed to the church at Thessalonica to commend them on their work of spreading the word of Jesus, and urges them to lead holy lives.

The Thunder, Perfect Mind—Gnostic text written in the first person by an anonymous female author during the first four centuries A.D. It is a highly paradoxical examination of Gnostic beliefs.

Tibetan Book of the Dead (Bardo Thodol)—Buddhist text written by Padmasambhava, a Tibetan monk, during the eighth century A.D. It is a series of instructions to the dead for the journey they embark on after death. Literally meaning "liberation by hearing in Bardo (death)," it is still used as a part of ritual during funerals.

1 Timothy—Christian text written by the apostle Paul ca. A.D. 61–63. It is a letter written to Timothy, a friend and convert of Paul, regarding the course of the Church and its followers.

2 Timothy—Christian text written by the apostle Paul ca. A.D. 66–67. It is a second letter to Timothy, urging him to promote the gospel and retain faith in Jesus.

Tirukkural—Hindu text written by Tiruvalluvar, an Indian poet, during the first century A.D. Also read by Jains, it is highly regarded by Hindus and is often considered to be the fifth of the Vedas.

Titus—Christian text written by the apostle Paul ca. A.D. 63–65. It is a letter to Titus, one of Paul's converts, examining the concepts of faith, godliness, and salvation.

Tobit—Judaeo-Christian text written ca. 200 B.C. by an unknown author of Palestinian or Syrian origin. It is an ethical tale of Jewish exile at Ninevah, with good and evil spirits that teach morality.

Tripartite Tractate—Gnostic text written by an unknown author some time during the first four centuries A.D. It discusses the Gnostic views of the creation of the world, the fall of man from Eden, and the redemptive acts of Jesus.

Twelve Meditations—Jain text written by Kunda Kunda, an Indian sage, in the first century A.D. It studies the Jain concept of worldly suffering and the reasons for its occurrence.

Udana—Buddhist text compiled by an unknown author written no later than the fifth century A.D. Considered to be the Tibetan version of the Dhammapada, it is a beautiful combination of verse and prose composition.

Urabe-no-Kanekuni — Shinto text written by Urabe-no-Kanekuni, a Japanese poet, during the first millennium A.D. It is a poem used in conjunction with a deer's shoulder blade or a tortoise shell to predict the future, much like the I Ching.

Uttara-Dhyayana Sutra — Jain text compiled by an unknown author during the fifth century A.D. Said to have been the last sermon of Mahavira, it instructs young monks entering the Jain religion.

Vemana's Padyamula — Hindu text said to have been written by Vemana, a legendary Teluguan poet, during the fifteenth century A.D. It is a poem examining the subjects of monotheism and iconoclasm.

Vinaya-Pitaka — Buddhist text compiled by unknown authors in the third or second century B.C. It is a collection of 200 rules of graded severity for teaching Buddhist pupils the rules of discipline and organization of monkhood.

Vishnu-Purana — Hindu text written ca. A.D. 400 by an unknown author. It is a theological treatise discussing the teachings of Vishnu and Krishna.

Visuddhimagga — Buddhist text written by Buddhaghosa, an Indian sage, during the fifth century B.C. Written for monks, it studies the cultivation of moral and mental purity that leads to enlightenment.

Viveka Chidamani — Hindu text written by Siva-guna-yogi, an Indian sage of the seventeenth century A.D. It is a dialogue between teacher and student discussing the techniques by which *yoga* and *jnana* (knowledge) can be practiced and acquired.

The Voice of the Silence — Buddhist text compiled by an unknown Tibetan monk during the eighth or ninth century A.D. It is a compilation of proverbs and sayings handed down by previous Tibetan monks.

The Wisdom of Solomon — Judaeo-Christian text written by an anonymous Alexandrian Jew ca. 100 B.C. It examines the concepts of reward and punishment after death, the spirit of the Lord, and the duality of body and soul.

Yahya — Sufi text written by Yahya, an early Sufi teacher, before his death in 871. It discusses early Moslem interpretation of the Koran and Hadith.

Yajurveda — Hindu text written by an unknown author sometime in the second millennium B.C. Known as the Knowledge of Sacrifice, it is one of the four Vedas, used primarily as a hymn book by Hindu priests.

Yasna — Zoroastrian text compiled by the followers of Zoroaster in the early third century B.C. Originally a prayer-book of the Zoroastrians, it was compiled from ancient oral teachings.

Yoga Sutras of Patanjali — Hindu text written by Patanjali, an Indian sage, during his life (estimated between 820 and 300 B.C.). It examines the basic teachings of Raja-yoga (Royal Yoga), an intellectual discipline added to traditional physical yoga training.

Zechariah — Judaeo-Christian text written by Zechariah, a prophet and priest, from 520 to 480 B.C. It was written to encourage the people of Judah in the rebuilding of their Temple to expedite the coming of the Messiah.

Zohar — Kabbalah text compiled by Moses de Leon, a Spanish Jewish mystic, between A.D. 1280 and 1286. Said to have been copied from a text by Rabbi Shim'on, an Israeli teacher of the second century A.D., it examines the sefirot and the Creation Myth.

Zostrianos — Gnostic text written by Zostrianos, an unknown author, during the second or first centuries B.C. It is an examination of non–Christian Gnosticism with which many Neoplatonic authors were familiar.

Bibliography

'Abdu'l-Baha. *Selections from the Writings of 'Abdu'l-Baha.* Compiled by the Research Department of the Universal House of Justice. Haifa: Baha'i World Centre, 1978.

The Adi Granth, or the Holy Scripture of the Sikhs. Trans. Dr. E. Trumpp. London: W.H. Allen, 1877.

Al-Suhrwady, Allama Sir Abdulah Al-Manum. *The Sayings of Mohammed.* The Wisdom of the East series. London: John Murray, 1941.

Amrit Chandra Acharya. *The Sacred Books of the Jains: Purusharta-Siddhyupaya Vol. IV.* Lucknow: The Central Jaina Publishing House, 1933.

The Analects. Trans. D.C. Lau. New York: Penguin Books, 1979.

Anonymous. *The Lost Books of the Bible and The Forgotten Books of Eden.* Cleveland: The World Publishing Company, 1927.

Aston, W.G. *Shinto, the Way of the Gods.* London: Longmans, Green, 1905.

Baha'u'llah. *Epistle to the Son of the Wolf.* Trans. Shoghi Effendi. Rev. ed. Wilmette, IL: Baha'i Publishing Trust, 1953.

————. *Gleanings from the Writings of Baha'u'llah.* Trans. Shoghi Effendi. Rev. ed. Wilmette, Il: Baha'i Publishing Trust, 1952.

————. *Gleanings from the Writings of Baha'u'llah.* Trans. Shoghi Effendi. New York: Baha'i Publishing Committee, 1935.

————. *The Kitab-i-Iqan: The Book of Certitude.* Trans. Shoghi Effendi. Rev. ed. Wilmette, IL: Baha'i Publishing Trust, 1950.

Ballou, Robert O., ed. *The Bible of the World.* New York: The Viking Press, 1939.

Beal, S. *Texts from the Buddhist Canon (Dhammapada).* London: Trubner & Co. 1878.

The Bhagavad Gita. Trans. Juan Mascaro. New York: Penguin Books, 1962.

The Book of Enoch. Trans. Richard Laurence, LL.D. Thousand Oaks, CA: Artisan Sales, 1980.

The Book of Mormon. Trans. Joseph Smith, Jr. Salt Lake City: The Church of Jesus Christ of Latter-day Saints, 1981.

Bouquet, A.C. *Sacred Books of the World.* London: Penguin Books, 1954.

Boylan, Michael. *Hafez: Dance of Life.* Washington: Mage Publishers, 1987.

Brown, Brian and David McKay, eds. *The Story of Confucius*. Philadelphia, 1927.

Burtt, E.A., ed. *The Teachings of the Compassionate Buddha*. New York: New American Library, 1955.

Champion, Selwyn Gurney, M.D. *The Eleven Religions and Their Proverbial Lore*. New York: E.P. Dutton & Co., Inc., 1945.

Chuang-tzu. Trans. Herbert A. Giles. London: George Allen & Unwin Ltd., 1961.

Cohen, A. *Everyman's Talmud*. New York: E.P. Dutton, 1949.

Cohen, Edward, ed. *Buddhist Texts Through the Ages*. New York: Harper & Row, Publishers, 1954.

_____. *Buddhist Scriptures*. New York: Penguin Books, 1959.

Dan, Joseph, ed. *The Early Kabbalah*. New York: Paulist Press, 1986.

Dawson, Miles Menander. *The Ethical Religion of Zoroaster*. New York: AMS Press, 1969.

The Dead Sea Scriptures. Trans. Theodor H. Gaster. Garden City: Anchor Books, 1964.

The Dhammapada. Trans. Irving Babbitt. New York: Oxford University Press, 1936.

The Dhammapada: The Path of Perfection. Trans. Juan Mascaro. New York: Penguin Books, 1973.

Epstein, Rabbi Dr. I. *The Babylonian Talmud*. 11 vols. London: Sonico Press, 1948.

Frost, S.E., ed. *The Sacred Writings of the World's Great Religions*. New York: McGraw-Hill Book Company, 1943.

Gaer, Joseph. *The Wisdom of the Living Religions*. New York: Dodd, Mead & Company, 1956.

Giles, Lionel. *The Sayings of Lao-Tzu*. Wisdom of the East series; American ed. New York: E.P. Dutton, 1908.

Hershon, P.I. *A Talmudic Miscelleny*. London: Trubner & Co., 1880.

Hitopadesa: The Book of Wholesome Counsel. Trans. by Francis Johnson; ed. by Lionel Barnett. London: Chapman and Hall, 1923.

Holy Bible: New International Version. New York: New York International Bible Society, 1978.

Holy Bible: The Open Bible Version. Nashville: Thomas Nelson Inc., Publishers, 1975.

Hume, Robert Ernest, ed. *Treasure-House of the Living Religions*. New York: Charles Scribner's Sons, 1933.

Hymms from the Rig Veda. Trans. Jean Marie Alexander Le Mee. New York: Alfred A. Knopf, Inc., 1975.

I Ching. Trans. Kerson and Rosemary Huang. New York: Workman Publishing, 1987.

Jatakas. Trans. and ed. by E.B. Cowell. London: Cambridge University Press, 1895.

Johnson, Clive, ed. *Vedanta: An Anthology of Hindu Scripture, Commentary and Poetry*. New York: Harper & Row, Publishers, 1971.

The Koran. Trans. N.J. Dagwood, New York: Penguin Books, 1956.

Lamza, George M., ed. *The Short Koran.* Chicago: Ziff-Davis Publishing Co., 1949.

The Lord's Song, or Bhagavad Gita. Trans. A. Besant. Madras: Nateson, 1932.

Macauliffe, Max Arthur. *The Sikh Religion.* 6 vols. Oxford: Clarendon Press, 1909.

Macintosh, W. *Gleanings from the Talmud.* London: Swan Sonnenschein, 1905.

McLeod, W.H. *Textual Sources for the Study of Sikhism.* Manchester: Manchester University Press, 1984.

The Mahabharata. 18 vols. Trans. J.A.B. van Buitenen. Chicago: The University of Chicago Press, 1973.

Malandra, William W. *An Introduction to Ancient Iranian Religion.* Minneapolis: University of Minnesota Press, 1983.

May, Herbert G. and Bruce M. Metzger, eds. *The New Oxford Annotated Bible with the Apocrypha.* New York: Oxford University Press, 1973.

Mead, Frank S., ed. *The Encyclopedia of Religious Quotations.* Westwood, N.J.: Fleming H. Revell Company, 1965.

Muller, Max, ed. *Sacred Books of the East.* Vols 1–50. Oxford: Clarendon Press, 1879–1910.

The Odes of Solomon. Trans. James Hamilton Charlesworth. Missoula, Montana: Scholars Press, 1977.

The Panchatantra. Trans. Arthur W. Ryder. Chicago: The University of Chicago Press, 1925.

The Platform Sutra of the Sixth Patriarch. Trans. Phillip B. Yampolsky. New York: Columbia University Press, 1967.

Prasad Sital. *Twelve Meditations, by Kunda Kunda.* Madras: Devendra Printing and Publishing Co., 1931.

The Rig Veda: An Anthology. Trans. Wendy Doniger O'Flaherty. New York: Penguin Books, 1981.

Robinson, James M., ed. *The Nag Hammadi Library.* San Francisco: Harper & Row, Publishers, 1978.

Rockhill, W.W. *Udanavarga: A Collection of Verses from the Buddhist Canon.* London: Trubner & Co., 1883.

The Samaveda. Trans. Devi Chand. New Delhi: Munshiram Manoharlal Publishers Pvt. Ltd., 1981.

Sandmel, Samuel, ed. *The New English Bible with the Apocrypha: Oxford Study Edition.* New York: Oxford University Press, 1976.

Sayings of the Fathers. Trans. by Joseph H. Hertz. New York: Behrman House, 1945.

Smart, Ninian, and Richard D. Hecht, eds. *Sacred Texts of the World: A Universal Anthology.* New York: Crossroad, 1982.

The Song Celestial (The Bhagavad Gita). Trans. Sir Edwin Arnold. Boston: Roberts, 1895.

Songs of Kabir. Trans. Rabindranath Tagore. New York: The Macmillan Company, 1916.

Suzuki, Daisetz Teitaro. *Manual of Zen Buddhism.* New York: Grove Press, Inc., 1960.

_____ and Carus, P. *Tai-Shang-Kan-Ying-Pien* Chicago: Open Court Co., 1906.

Tao Teh Ching. Trans. Chu Ta-Kao. London: The Buddhist Lodge, 1937.

Tao Teh Ching. Trans. Steven Mitchell. New York: Harper & Row, 1988.

Tao Teh Ch'ing. Trans. W.G. Old and W.L. Hare. London: C.W. Daniels, N.D.

The Texts of the White Yajurveda. Trans. Ralph T.H. Griffith. New Delhi: Munshiram Manoharlal Publishers Private Limited, 1987.

Thomas, E.J. *The Song of the Lord: Bhagavad Gita.* Wisdom of The East. London: J. Murray, 1931.

The Tibetan Book of the Dead. Trans. Frank J. MacHovec. Mount Vernon, New York: Peter Pauper Press, 1972.

Two Zen Classics: Mumonkan and Hekiganroku. Trans. Katsuki Sekida. New York: Weatherhill, 1977.

The Upanishads. Trans. Juan Mascaro. New York: Penguin Books, 1965.

Waley, Arthur. *The Way and Its Power.* London: G. Allen and Unwin, 1934.

The Way of Life. Trans. Witter Bynner. New York: Capricorn Books, 1944.

Woodward, F.L. *Some Sayings of the Buddha According to the Pali Canon.* London: Oxford University Press, 1973.

Yutang, Lin. *The Wisdom of China and India.* New York: The Modern Library, 1955.

_____. *The Wisdom of Confucius.* New York. The Modern Library, 1938.

_____. *The Wisdom of Laotse.* New York: The Modern Library, 1948.

Zohar: The Book of Enlightenment. Trans. Daniel Chanan Matt. New York: Paulist Press, 1983.

Index by Religion
and Source

Baha'i
The Book of Certitude 887, 932
Epistle to the Son of the
   Wolf 105, 228
Gleanings from the Writings of
   Baha'u'llah 133, 182, 404, 463,
   479, 633, 658, 676, 874, 1007,
   1043, 1050, 1066, 1126, 1186, 1355,
   1400, 1483, 1511, 1615
Selections from the Writings of
   'Abdu'l Baha 39, 980

Buddhism
Anguttara-Nikaya 10, 317, 560,
   936
Asoka's Edicts 1645
The Awakening of Faith 1084,
   1086
Bodhicaryavatara 1440
Buddha-Karita 1083
Bya Chos 583, 590, 868, 1434
Dhammapada 61, 88, 161, 168,
   220, 310, 331, 358, 365, 372, 380,
   384, 397, 492, 495, 498, 504, 567,
   691, 703, 717, 720, 729, 750, 756,
   762, 765, 769, 776, 855, 907,
   1016, 1023, 1026, 1033, 1063, 1073,
   1092, 1107, 1110, 1239, 1253, 1294,
   1298, 1314, 1359, 1418, 1467, 1514,
   1530, 1583, 1605, 1620
Dharmapada 181, 375
Digha Nikaya 171
Diamond Sutra 637, 1570

Fo-Sho-Hing-Tsan-King 786,
   1398
Jatakas 126, 337, 487, 501, 535,
   774, 1125, 1135, 1285
Itu-vuttaka 253, 545, 574, 1070,
   1518
Lalitavistara 1493
Lankavatara Sutra 203
Lotus Sutra 206, 217
Mahavagga 114, 520, 1030, 1114,
   1272, 1312
Majjhima-Nikaya 754, 883, 1265
Mila Grubum 49, 91, 118, 129, 184,
   270, 288, 346, 467, 841, 1020, 1121,
   1181, 1308, 1498
Milindapanha 1236
The Ocean of Delight for the
   Wise 266, 739
Ratnagotravibhaga 1444
Samyutta-Nikaya 33, 246, 303,
   1328, 1412
Saraha's Treasury of Songs 78,
   283, 307, 355, 914, 922, 944,
   1094, 1101, 1104, 1303, 1490, 1503
Satapancasatkastotra 107
Shrichakrasambhara Tantra 1089,
   1171
The Staff of Wisdom 661, 1056
Subhashita Ratna Nidhi 68, 743,
   1545
Sutta-Nipata 409, 417, 444, 462,
   734, 1629
Tibetan Book of the Dead 137,
   140, 145, 243, 421, 688, 863, 1011,

1078, 1098, 1205, 1316, 1408, 1428,
1481, 1590
Udana 576, 671, 1165, 1322
Vinaya Pitaka 1342
Visuddhimagga 724
The Voice of the Silence 73, 1318,
1339

Christianity
The Bible—New Testament
Acts 424, 565, 597, 1065
Colossians 461
1 Corinthians 15, 40, 138, 190,
205, 511, 609, 852, 894, 976,
984, 994, 1014, 1491, 1497,
1593
2 Corinthians 394, 568, 592, 1151,
1465
Ephesians 775, 1237, 1271, 1485,
1501
Galatians 247, 401, 680, 1017,
1025, 1353, 1357, 1504
Hebrews 262, 277, 385, 642, 708,
1280
James 3, 160, 202, 223, 231, 319,
330, 356, 391, 571, 933, 1203,
1368, 1558
John 37, 388, 553, 736, 757, 840,
856, 959, 1008, 1289, 1364, 1448,
1640
1 John 603, 606, 990, 996, 1002,
1010, 1233, 1604, 1619
3 John 1471
Luke 480, 518, 521, 530, 577,
663, 875, 1172, 1193, 1195, 1297,
1401, 1628
Mark 474, 782
Matthew 26, 34, 74, 196, 235,
353, 478, 515, 559, 573, 580,
627, 659, 677, 698, 789, 816,
867, 873, 906, 950, 955, 1037,
1141, 1166, 1197, 1206, 1221, 1240,
1266, 1279, 1335, 1393, 1541,
1548, 1612, 1631
1 Peter 90, 219, 832, 1105, 1410,
1420, 1423
2 Peter 1115
Philippians 183, 836, 1127, 1250
Romans 82, 121, 167, 315, 411,
588, 653, 667, 692, 869, 981,
1006, 1097, 1102, 1362, 1374,
1429
1 Thessalonians 1212, 1247
1 Timothy 370, 1191
2 Timothy 926
Titus 106, 305
The Bible—New Testament
Apocrypha
Acts of John 1426
Epistle of Ignatius to the
Ephesians 300
Epistle of Ignatius to the
Philadelphians 45
Epistle of Ignatius to
Polycarp 1588
The First Epistle of Clement to
the Corinthians 268, 686, 847,
1573
The Odes of Solomon 92, 902,
1155, 1187, 1563
Isaac of Ninevah 1189
Logia 66, 523, 974, 1610
New Sayings of Jesus 1311
The Bible—Old Testament see
Judaism
The Bible—Old Testament
Apocrypha see Judaism

Confucianism
The Analects 18, 22, 51, 54, 57,
60, 63, 67, 70, 76, 86, 96, 99,
104, 113, 186, 188, 216, 269, 272,
284, 299, 301, 306, 312, 314, 321,
333, 336, 347, 351, 354, 357, 361,
387, 489, 510, 522, 526, 533, 547,
552, 584, 670, 709, 732, 741, 748,
773, 791, 817, 866, 885, 910, 915,
927, 938, 945, 947, 953, 958, 971,
1029, 1051, 1074, 1113, 1128, 1164,
1168, 1184, 1202, 1230, 1242, 1245,
1254, 1345, 1363, 1439, 1447, 1475,
1506, 1522, 1542, 1552, 1589, 1594
The Book of Filial Piety 1148
Doctrine of the Mean 292, 1144,
1327, 1354

The Great Learning 457, 1513
Li Ki 2234, 964, 1064, 1067, 1122,
1358, 1510, 1517, 1634, 442, 450,
690, 738, 778, 827, 962, 968, 973,
979, 982, 985, 1042, 1044, 1061,
1108, 1321, 1488
Shih King 59, 448
Shu King 5, 142, 297, 339,
502, 598, 694, 821, 851, 1116,
1283
Sun Yi-jang 1341

Gnosticism
The Book of Thomas the
Contender 1035
The Dialogue of the Saviour 198
Gospel of Phillip 31, 239, 273,
986, 1199, 1489
Gospel of Truth 1340
On the Origin of the World 52
The Second Apocalypse of James
854
The Sentences of Sextus 101, 130,
178, 413, 802, 908, 935, 998, 1022,
1185, 1349, 1468, 1625
The Teachings of Silvanius 43,
308, 551, 601, 644, 649, 871, 1309
The Thunder, Perfect Mind 655,
1302
Tripartite Tractate 611, 617, 640
Zostrianos 1231

Hinduism
Aitareya Brahmana 465
Anugita 801
Ashtavakra Gita 1096, 1445
Atharva Veda 1214
Bani 46
Bhagavad Gita 6, 21, 53, 116, 127,
134, 177, 199, 209, 212, 215, 224,
378, 389, 496, 591, 607, 612, 647,
651, 696, 917, 965, 983, 1015, 1018,
1024, 1143, 1196, 1232, 1275, 1287,
1291, 1330, 1407, 1421, 1427, 1462,
1473, 1492, 1579, 1582, 1587, 1592,
1601, 1642

Bhagavata Purana 30, 877, 975,
995, 1013, 1477, 1505, 1630
Bharavi's Kiratarjuniya 727
Brihad-Aranyaka Upanishad 191,
395, 654
Chandogya Upanishad 407, 419,
779, 1268, 1450
Garuda Purana 38, 236, 251, 343,
446, 532, 536, 731, 737, 745, 886,
893, 898, 989, 1130, 1152, 1404,
1415
Hathayoga Pradipka 1436
Hitopadesa 16, 84, 189, 254, 290,
426, 431, 452, 472, 508, 542, 549,
564, 579, 669, 711, 1039, 1103,
1182, 1441, 1581
Isha Upanishad 901, 1293, 1486,
1500
Katha Upanishad 700, 809, 1300,
1495, 1534
Kaushitaki Upanishad 1079
Knowledge of Spirit 28
Laws of Manu 221, 433, 752, 767,
853, 864, 930, 941, 1118, 1296,
1320
Mahabharata 64, 71, 131, 248, 519,
524, 558, 572, 657, 660, 665, 682,
719, 812, 951, 1071, 1075, 1100,
1188, 1192, 1228, 1348
Mahanirvana Tantra 1638
Maitri Upanishad 625, 638, 1082,
1093
Markandeya Purana 1159
Mundaka Upanishad 621, 634,
1109, 1480
Narada Smriti 437
Panchatantra 174, 232, 240, 678,
707, 946, 1305, 1453, 1521, 1531,
1562, 1572
Ramayana 1047, 1456
Rig Veda 516, 1059, 1261, 1333
Samaveda 749, 880, 1090, 1402
Sarva-Darsana-Samgraha 1027
Satapatha Brahmana 1365, 1633
The Sayings of Sri Ramakrishna
11, 75, 81, 218, 352, 398, 722, 798,
805, 904, 993, 1001, 1087, 1163,
1536, 1627, 1636, 1644

Srimad Bhagavatam 1639
The Supreme Teaching 229
Svetasvatara Upanishad 602, 615,
    1385, 1425
Taittiriya Upanishad 569, 594
Tirukkural 166, 325, 1343, 1525
Vemana's Padyamula xii, 1646
Vishnu Purana 675, 1053
Viveka Chidamani 194
Yajurveda 329, 414, 889
Yoga Sutras of Patanjani 1338,
    1392

Islam
The Forty-Two Traditions of An-
    Nawawi 318
Hadith 12, 19, 44, 69, 123, 225,
    233, 368, 371, 392, 410, 455, 469,
    664, 806, 833, 899, 1036, 1057,
    1220, 1255, 1304, 1334, 1344, 1414,
    1451, 1460, 1523, 1549, 1597, 1607,
    1618
Koran 79, 97, 165, 187, 214, 244,
    256, 267, 338, 350, 362, 381, 406,
    412, 418, 430, 447, 482, 513, 517,
    554, 570, 587, 605, 613, 628, 681,
    687, 704, 747, 771, 857, 859, 921,
    1041, 1077, 1124, 1204, 1210, 1217,
    1225, 1270, 1273, 1276, 1284, 1288,
    1369, 1375, 1381, 1383, 1387, 1396,
    1406, 1585, 1602
Mishkat-el-Masabih 453, 557,
    645, 668, 710, 839

Jainism
Acharanga Sutra 541, 788, 956,
    1140, 1449, 1455, 1556
Avesyaka Sutra 529
Dasaveyaliya 684
Nirgrantha-Pravachana 192, 207
Paramatma-prakasha 1388
Pravacana-sara 367, 890
Samadhi Shataka 136
Siri-siri-valaka 561
Sutra-krit-anga 65, 349, 423, 443,
    473, 507, 662, 716, 831, 842, 1068,

1085, 1132, 1150, 1167, 1178, 1229,
    1234, 1243, 1251, 1258, 1299, 1367,
    1379, 1416, 1466, 1507, 1568, 1596,
    1606, 1613
Tattvartha Sutra 386
Twelve Meditations 14
Uttara-Dhyayana Sutra 2, 20,
    222, 274, 723, 753, 759, 766, 925,
    977, 1034, 1224, 1238, 1306, 1520,
    1547, 1623

Judaism
The Bible – Old Testament
    Amos 683
    Deuteronomy 639
    Ecclesiastes 128, 250, 334, 464,
        506, 537, 548, 715, 721, 725,
        811, 916, 1049, 1088, 1158, 1319,
        1544, 1554, 1575, 1593, 1637
    Exodus 434, 1346
    Ezekiel 1080, 1389
    Genesis 359
    Habakkuk 416, 764
    Haggai 95
    Isaiah 77, 193, 471, 619, 1175, 1244
    Jeremiah 784, 1286
    Job 147, 260, 282, 322, 363, 366,
        1069, 1378, 1565, 1569
    Judges 62
    Leviticus 1000
    Malachi 1257
    Numbers 1372
    Proverbs 55, 87, 98, 109, 112, 132,
        155, 158, 163, 210, 241, 257, 265,
        271, 280, 311, 316, 326, 405,
        422, 436, 445, 451, 454, 458,
        486, 488, 497, 503, 509, 540,
        636, 695, 705, 712, 718, 730,
        777, 780, 796, 799, 804, 820,
        825, 843, 850, 860, 879, 882,
        888, 913, 920, 931, 937, 940,
        943, 963, 967, 970, 992, 1012,
        1031, 1076, 1112, 1117, 1131, 1209,
        1274, 1323, 1329, 1397, 1529,
        1535, 1538, 1561, 1600
    Psalms 483, 500, 585, 689, 742,
        768, 1046, 1055, 1072, 1438

1 Samuel 25, 340
Song of Solomon 1004
Zechariah 1452
The Bible—Old Testament
  Apocrypha
Ecclesiasticus 103, 117, 135, 150,
  287, 291, 324, 332, 344, 373,
  429, 439, 441, 470, 491, 494,
  525, 531, 543, 733, 760, 792,
  822, 928, 1120, 1136, 1262, 1332,
  1370, 1380, 1382, 1454, 1458,
  1546, 1551, 1557, 1571, 1578
Tobit 170
The Wisdom of Solomon 1516,
  1567, 1580, 1584
Dead Sea Scrolls
The Manual of Discipline 180,
  255, 631, 1052
The Book of Enoch 23, 152, 1376
Rokeach 527
The Sayings of the Fathers 7,
  125, 296, 313, 328, 830, 858,
  876, 1282, 1533, 1559, 1591, 1608
Talmud 29, 144, 176, 200, 208,
  258, 279, 293, 298, 302, 379,
  403, 420, 427, 432, 456, 460,
  466, 476, 534, 556, 562, 595,
  623, 679, 701, 746, 772, 794,
  807, 810, 814, 834, 846, 862,
  911, 1058, 1062, 1161, 1180, 1200,
  1215, 1219, 1223, 1226, 1269,
  1292, 1326, 1360, 1366, 1384,
  1386, 1413, 1463, 1509, 1598,
  1614, 1621

Kabbalah
The Book of Faith and Reliance
  408
Zohar 383, 652, 673, 1156, 1173,
  1331, 1395, 1479, 1577

Mormonism
Alma 818
Doctrines and Covenants 399,
  614, 905, 1252, 1474
Helaman 376
Moroni 582, 865

Shinto
Chucho-Jijitsu 1211
Gorikai 27, 35, 141, 415, 624, 630,
  648, 758, 770, 808, 1213, 1411,
  1422, 1435
Kojiki 237, 783, 1241, 1472
Munetada 1060, 1609, 1624
Nihongi 159, 164, 320, 341, 382,
  402, 505, 795, 949, 1281, 1550
Oracle of Hachiman 589, 1603
Oracle of Tatsuta 1208
Oracle of the Deity Atsuta 440
An Oracle of the Deity
  Temmangu 278
Oracle of the Gods of Kasuga 58,
  813
Urabe-no-Kanekuni 635

Sikhism
Adi Granth 17, 48, 110, 139, 153,
  226, 230, 242, 245, 323, 369, 390,
  425, 459, 481, 499, 575, 581, 596,
  629, 641, 650, 672, 693, 697, 726,
  728, 740, 761, 781, 787, 790, 803,
  845, 848, 923, 987, 1028, 1038,
  1045, 1091, 1216, 1222, 1256, 1373,
  1424, 1442, 1461, 1469, 1476, 1512,
  1528, 1555, 1564, 1599, 1617, 1632,
  1635, 1643
Asa Ki War 120, 201, 550, 714,
  1278, 1352, 1457, 1641
Dasam Granth 620, 1040, 1048,
  1176, 1405, 1482
Gobind Singh 1133
Hymns of Guru Nanak 285, 393,
  861
Japji Granth 616, 897
Kabir's Sloks 528, 797, 1539
Kirtan Sohila 490
Namhardi Rahit-nama 514
Shaikh Brahm 1267
Sloks of Shaikh Farid 24, 793
Sohar Rahiras 600
Songs of Kabir 32, 42, 172, 646,
  919, 991, 997, 1147
Sukhmani 477

Sufism
Book of Wisdom 8, 169, 249, 263,
  586, 815, 891, 1005, 1201, 1246,
  1263, 1419
Divan 1394, 1626
Gulshan i-Rza 1019, 1446, 1464,
  1553, 1611
Hazrat Ali 593
Intimate Conversations 544
Masnavi 546, 800, 1431
Song of the Dervish 4, 835, 1003,
  1260
Yahya 999

Taoism Chou-ilueh-li 345
Chuang-tzu 50, 56, 115, 122, 146,
  204, 294, 360, 512, 599, 608, 643,
  785, 872, 881, 884, 900, 903, 942,
  966, 1021, 1095, 1123, 1139, 1149,
  1157, 1160, 1177, 1183, 1194, 1290,
  1307, 1310, 1317, 1324, 1502, 1524
I Ching 89, 151, 261, 276, 485,
  555, 578, 838, 1129, 1207
Lieh Tzu 1443
Saikondan 1153
T'ai Shang Kan Ying P'ien 327,
  335, 666, 699, 751
Tao Teh Ching 1, 9, 36, 72, 102,
  111, 119, 143, 173, 185, 195, 213, 281,
  304, 309, 348, 377, 396, 400, 435,
  475, 493, 539, 604, 618, 626, 632,
  685, 706, 713, 744, 755, 763, 819,
  823, 829, 837, 878, 892, 895, 909,
  948, 952, 954, 957, 960, 969,
  1009, 1054, 1111, 1134, 1137, 1142,
  1146, 1154, 1162, 1190, 1198, 1227,
1248, 1295, 1313, 1315, 1347, 1351,
  1409, 1484, 1508, 1515, 1519, 1527,
  1622

Zen
Hekiganroku 149, 157, 259, 824,
  844, 918, 1138, 1325, 1336, 1350,
  1487, 1540
Mumonkan 94, 162, 264, 912, 929,
  934, 939, 1106, 1145, 1179, 1301,
  1430, 1433
On Trust in the Heart 154, 286,
  622, 1174, 1459, 1478, 1496,
  1574
Shijin-no-mei 1499
Song of Enlightenment 1081
Song of Meditation 1361
Tan Ching 47, 80, 197, 342, 1032,
  1169, 1249, 1437, 1566

Zoroastrianism
Avesta 83, 124, 468, 563, 566,
  702, 735, 896, 972, 1235, 1356,
  1432, 1526, 1537
Dadistan-i-dinik 656, 849, 1119,
  1377
Dinkard 179, 826, 1371
Fragments of the Nasks 139
Menog-i Khrad 252, 484, 1576
Pand Nameh 538
Sad Dar 1470
Shayast-na-shayast 100, 175, 238,
  674, 1586
Yasna 156, 211, 374, 428, 438, 610,
  870, 1099, 1218, 1264, 1277, 1399

Index by Key Words and Topics

Abhor 436, 860
Ability 70, 1164, 1184
Abstention 1118
Abundance 569, 725, 1195, 1386
Abuse 64, 665
Achieve, achievement 56, 143, 184, 331, 398, 426
Act, acts *see* Action
Action 1–25, 59, 97–98, 101, 148, 170, 275, 340, 362, 376, 468, 498, 610, 668, 675, 695, 699, 805, 901, 910, 938, 1010, 1092, 1121, 1234, 1251, 1272, 1278, 1367, 1427, 1548, 1638
Adultery 782, 1036–1037
Advice xiii, 158
Affection *see* Love
Afraid *see* Fear
Afterlife beyond 417, 419, 638, 779
Ail *see* Disease
All 113, 116, 212, 250, 499, 811, 812, 1444, 1462, 1482, 1494, 1496
Allah *see* God
Almighty *see* God
Alms 557, 570, 574, 587, 1210, 1273
Ambition 183, 319, 328, 330, 1247
Amend *see* Correct
Angel 1019
Anger 88, 110, 378, 524, 760–761, 770, 774, 1075, 1253
Angry 513, 759, 766–768, 1075, 1096
Animals 367, 654, 1053, 1075; bear 503; beast 1053, 1055–1056;

birds 1454; cats 745; creatures 253, 662, 1182, 1296, 1300, 1416; cubs 503; dog 323, 1019; frogs 1373; gnat 834, 1553; hare 1033; horse 94, 259, 918, 972, 1320; sheep 959, 1050; spider 654
Another *see* Others
Answer 1319, 1323
Argue 102, 104, 162
Arms *see* Body
Assets *see* Wealth
Atonement 570, 1370, 1384, 1413

Babe *see* Children
Bad 250, 304, 382, 697, 703, 1057, 1408, 1586
Battle *see* War
Bear *see* Animals
Beast *see* Animals
Beauty 32, 327, 1074, 1562; beautiful 527, 917
Beer *see* Drink
Begging 572, 842
Beginning 114, 122, 242, 263, 293, 472, 488, 620, 641, 1246, 1580
Behavior 113; attitude 141
Belief, believe 386, 388, 420, 435, 474, 624, 1206, 1273
Believer 415, 664, 1549
Bellies *see* Body
Belong *see* Possessions

Benefit 184, 228, 1341
Benevolence 54, 309, 442, 552, 791, 979, 1386
Beyond see Afterlife
Birds see Animals
Birth, born 14, 115–116, 118–120, 122, 194, 209, 223, 246, 378, 441, 465, 540, 638, 803, 885, 1069, 1232, 1265, 1296, 1550; cradle 899
Blame 61, 68, 347–349, 815, 1458
Blessed 260, 388, 406, 483, 565, 699, 700, 802, 1007, 1410, 1417
Blessing 325, 581, 1434, 1629
Bliss see Happiness
Body 14, 26–50, 136, 194, 326, 478, 480, 611, 733, 1105, 1373, 1403, 1414, 1420, 1490, 1497, 1501, 1553, 1567, 1616; arms 741, 1150; bellies 44; bones 326, 451, 470, 1343; ear 73, 619, 988, 1326, 1329, 1332, 1336–1337; eye xi, 27, 41, 193, 266, 332, 343, 449, 619, 621, 712, 806, 844, 988, 1036; 1215, 1286, 1326–1327; 1329, 1479, 1643; face 133, 796, 804, 832; feet 432, 469, 807, 1340; fingers 232; flesh 27, 31, 37, 46, 1241, 1391; forehead 244; hair 383; hands 509, 559, 1247, 1340; head 1061; lips 497, 758, 943, 1274, 1479; liver 44; mouth 808, 828, 924, 1166, 1274, 1378; tongue 714, 913, 931–933, 937, 1010, 1036, 1328, 1378, 1433, 1479
Bondage 88, 590, 868, 1082, 1093, 1096, 1303, 1434
Bones see Body
Books see Scripture
Breath 174, 230, 249, 1072
Brother 123, 448–449, 536, 540, 664, 873, 1060, 1489
Building see Home

Carnal 1097, 1118
Cats see Animals
Celebration: cheer 68; rejoice 64, 617, 742, 1279; revelry 1374
Change 74, 238, 284, 1190
Character 51–70, 105, 451
Charity 392, 561, 570, 589, 921, 1508, 1545
Chastity 739
Cheer see Celebration
Child see Children
Children 71–85, 639, 1163, 1471; babe 212; child 71, 73, 77–78, 81, 98, 280, 446; childlike 1404; offspring 468
Choice see Decision
Church: mosque 1176; temple 45, 1176
City 32, 1131
Clothes 761, 1112, 1194
Compassion see Love
Complacency, smug 93, 97, 113
Conceal 341, 358; hide, hidden 430, 548, 633, 646, 711, 1012, 1144, 1170, 1300–1301, 1571
Conceit 183, 288, 378
Conduct 86–113, 1224, 1238, 1243
Conquer 1306, 1407
Control 1100, 1299; self-control 106, 1131
Converse see Language
Correct 265, 268, 271, 301, 306, 341, 849; amend, mend 333, 336, 351, 1375; improve 826; reform 357
Courage 18, 54, 113
Covets see Envy
Cradle see Birth
Create 610, 834–835, 880, 1066, 1077, 1110, 1436, 1482, 1563
Creator 251, 887, 1066 see God
Creatures see Animals
Crime 335, 339, 1366
Cubs see Animals
Cupidity see Love
Curse 518, 1123, 1307

Damnation 376
Dangerous see Trouble
Darkness, dark 191, 199, 651, 1489

Daughter 464
Day xi, 124, 742, 754, 1072, 1384, 1425; today 254; tomorrow 231, 235, 1100; yesterday 254, 1110
Dead, deadly see Death
Death 114–146, 174, 191, 223, 246, 328, 398–399, 417, 484, 901, 931, 1004, 1097, 1360, 1374, 1489, 1495, 1605; dead 126, 391, 1159; deadly 932; die 115–116, 119–120, 127, 134–135, 166, 1296, 1389; grave 899
Deceit, deception 190, 196, 202, 378, 782, 784, 933, 1229
Decision 147–164, 861; choice 149, 151–152, 154, 156, 161, 316, 511, 700, 1113
Deed, deeds 10, 52, 165–189, 375, 433, 498, 691, 826, 946, 1235, 1283, 1296, 1375, 1451, 1639
Deity see God
Delusion 171, 190–209, 1063, 1486
Desire 58, 171, 207, 209–229, 661, 670, 676, 684, 803, 813, 896, 1019, 1025, 1082, 1096, 1196, 1227, 1284, 1332, 1388, 1467, 1580, 1587, 1619
Destiny 230–257
Destruction, destroy 166, 384, 438, 450, 712, 720, 850, 1017, 1160, 1197, 1301, 1361
Devotion, devout 740, 1200, 1277, 1570
Die see Death
Difficult 5, 154, 703, 785, 1294, 1345
Discipline 258–280, 488
Disease, sick, ail 33, 36, 195, 226, 728, 892, 1026, 1042, 1472, 1507
Divine 56, 69, 81, 238, 897, 1021, 1034, 1211
Dog see Animals
Door 359, 878, 1201, 1221, 1255, 1266, 1309; gate 270
Dream see Sleep
Drink 1118–1119, 1124, 1132, 1135–1136; beer 1117; liquor 1118; wine 1117, 1120, 1136, 1578
Drowsiness see Sleep
Drunk 1217; drunkard 509, 1112, 1163

Dust 128, 212, 724
Duty 224, 1590, 1592

Ear see Body
Earth see Nature, earth
Earthly 224, 1603
Eat 230, 498, 741, 1056, 1118, 1124, 1128, 1132, 1135
Education 281–315, 446, 463; learn xii, 289, 292–293, 295–298, 303, 311, 314, 431, 960, 1125, 1313, 1468, 1580, 1590; learned 100; teach xii, xiii, 106, 173, 179, 282–283, 285, 290, 295–298, 300, 305, 310, 313, 315, 355, 1239; teacher 278, 285, 299, 302, 308–309, 314, 364, 685, 801, 975, 1064, 1579
Effort 547, 637, 1305, 1522
Egoism see Pride
Emotion 737
End 114, 122, 131, 142, 263, 324, 348, 616, 620, 641, 716, 1027, 1228, 1246, 1291, 1380–1382, 1384, 1398, 1425, 1435, 1441, 1589
Enemies 100, 166, 446, 535, 548, 554, 659, 720, 801, 1107, 1407; foe 556
Enjoyment see Happiness
Enslaved see Slave
Envy 110, 125, 316–332, 782, 976, 1380; jealousy 787; covet 323, 329, 790, 1152
Equal xiii, 272, 441, 448, 628, 821, 1183, 1254, 1447
Error 198, 313, 333–361, 1473; mistake 339, 351–352; wrong 149, 157, 159, 162, 171, 174, 282, 338, 341–342, 344, 354, 381, 527, 703, 771, 865, 992, 1107, 1148, 1157, 1251, 1540, 1589
Escape 166, 291, 1324
Essence 13, 1084, 1371, 1400
Eternal see Immortality
Everlasting see Immortality
Everyone 69, 90, 1271

202   Index by Key Words

Everything 139, 238, 596, 603, 930,
984, 1022, 1198–1199, 1461, 1493,
1527, 1634
Evil 109, 165, 168, 171, 177, 181, 210,
319–320, 362–384, 490, 554, 582,
667, 681–682, 686–687, 689,
692–693, 705, 768, 782, 791, 1225,
1423, 1430
Excess 707, 1116, 1122–1126, 1134,
1229, 1371
Existence 14, 30, 251, 1084, 1526,
1586
Experience 145, 1344
Eye see Body

Face see Body
Failure, fail 13, 36, 70, 194, 266,
341, 446, 472, 701, 1164, 1184, 1213
Faith xii, 3, 106, 385–419, 561, 567,
839, 986, 1115, 1216, 1219, 1224,
1236, 1238, 1243, 1257, 1404, 1485,
1642; faithful 1468, 1607;
reliance 405, 408
Falsehood 420–439, 484, 714, 941,
1479; fraud 684
Family 440–470; relatives 557
Fate 232, 236, 240, 248, 251
Father 440, 443–445, 464, 515, 902,
951, 1064, 1148, 1221, 1604
Faults 94, 309, 334–337, 343,
356, 358, 814, 866, 868, 1242,
1359
Fear 31, 42, 130, 171, 471–490, 496,
843, 891, 968, 974, 1056, 1071,
1250, 1293; afraid 54, 143, 351,
474, 478–479, 555, 1518
Feel see Senses
Feet see Body
Female see Woman
Fingers see Body
Fire 211, 380, 545–546, 654, 932,
1421
First 264, 310, 694, 757, 1075, 1141,
1185, 1364
Flesh see Body
Foe see Enemy

Folly see Foolishness
Food 897; apples 920; crops 963;
fish 948; loaf 1497; milk 168
Fool xi, 109, 150, 194, 210, 322, 340,
488, 491–512, 550, 1121, 1553,
1629
Foolishness, foolish 49, 445, 510,
535, 609, 716, 720, 1379; folly xi,
503, 508, 511, 782, 879, 1052,
1323, 1571; stupid 265, 284, 491,
1121, 1162
Forehead see Body
Forever see Immortality
Forgiving 513–530, 921, 1075, 1232,
1414
Fornication 40; copulating 1056;
intercourse 1035, 1118
Freedom, free 30, 35, 156, 224, 273,
325, 372, 417, 573, 749, 769, 788,
791, 914, 1030, 1078, 1082, 1105,
1232, 1238, 1314, 1448
Friendship 531–556; friend 100,
415, 531, 533–538, 540–544,
546–549, 551–556, 1214, 1407
Frogs see Animals
Fruits 14, 365, 408, 498, 931, 1015,
1172, 1285, 1288, 1584, 1596;
fruitful 169
Future 583, 620, 1167, 1437, 1439,
1586

Gain 53, 314, 321, 412, 666, 805,
886, 1228, 1269, 1538, 1540, 1612;
obtain 58, 753, 769, 813, 1083,
1278, 1481, 1527–1528
Gate see Door
Gift 49, 441, 564, 569, 572,
582–583, 591, 877, 1266, 1641
Giving, give 37, 223, 557–591, 812,
986, 1193, 1253, 1343, 1532
Gnats see Animals
God xi, xii, 24–25, 44–46, 58, 82,
133, 167, 180, 214–215, 218, 225–
226, 244, 260, 277, 285, 352–353,
415, 424, 463, 467, 479, 500, 511,
522, 528, 534, 568, 592–655, 738,

740, 751, 781, 798, 859, 904, 996,
1002, 1065–1066, 1090, 1099, 1102,
1180, 1233, 1246, 1253, 1256, 1267,
1290, 1297, 1304, 1346, 1362, 1400,
1421, 1425, 1442, 1456, 1460, 1469,
1477, 1504, 1528, 1541, 1558, 1582,
1593, 1601, 1625, 1630–1631, 1636,
1640; Allah 338; Almighty 260,
1644; Creator 1066; Deity xii,
635, 1211; He 586, 597, 607,
611–612, 615, 617, 620, 646–647,
651, 1124, 1263; Him 616, 621,
640, 1263, 1635, 1638; His 1187;
I 655, 1080; It 599, 622, 626,
632, 639; Lord 25, 40, 87, 112,
163, 241, 257, 262, 405, 436, 454,
477, 483, 486, 488, 566, 605, 610,
612, 636, 639, 843, 860–861, 1209,
1244, 1260, 1271, 1273, 1329, 1346,
1438, 1462, 1485, 1628, 1631, 1637;
Me 447, 604, 637, 983, 1642;
My 1043; One 858; One
Soul 654; Spirit 638, 1501;
Tao 618; We 1284
Godly, godliness 802, 998;
god-like 1404
Gods 1314, 1421, 1642
Gold xiii, 198, 546, 920, 1546
Golden Rule 656–679
Good xii, 51, 65, 92, 175–176,
184–185, 194, 250, 300, 304, 341,
362, 365, 402, 406, 428, 433, 454,
519, 533, 554, 570–571, 582, 656,
675, 680–705, 734, 747, 763, 780,
917 1057, 1099, 1114, 1225, 1239,
1271, 1273, 1348, 1368, 1423, 1430,
1510, 1544, 1552, 1583, 1585–1586,
1612
Grace 352, 581, 1237
Grave see Death
Great, greater 61, 75, 85, 175–176,
234, 325, 334, 468, 504, 512, 553,
575, 603, 640, 942, 1279, 1300,
1471, 1560, 1588, 1592;
greatest 100, 142, 1526
Greed 684, 706–726, 782, 1328
Grief, grieve 68, 130–131, 134, 1096,
1100, 1188, 1192, 1424, 1486;

misery 182, 438, 1415; weep 126,
742, 1286
Growth see Prosperity
Guilty 379, 520, 1381

Hair see Body
Hands see Body
Happiness 727–755, 1194, 1475;
bliss 406; cheerful 568; enjoyment 198, 749; happy 135, 542,
546, 719, 727, 730, 735, 744,
1030, 1096, 1399, 1514; joy 215,
445, 563, 569, 617, 732–733, 736,
747, 754, 799, 1092, 1419, 1471
Hare see Animals
Harm 1107, 1129, 1251, 1589;
hurt 525, 671, 729, 1107, 1316;
hurtful 679, 925
Harmony 738, 917, 1484
Hatred 125, 171, 209, 265, 321, 380,
545, 756–776, 992, 1011, 1063,
1107, 1500, 1574, 1588, 1591;
wrath 764, 768, 775, 790
Head see Body
Hear see Senses
Heart xii, xiii, 85, 92, 169, 215, 229,
241, 266, 326, 330, 500, 508, 543,
546, 591, 596, 603–604, 652, 733,
758, 761, 770, 777–810, 871, 911,
962, 974–975, 997, 1013, 1037–
1038, 1094, 1150, 1201, 1215, 1226,
1235, 1261, 1275, 1277, 1300, 1355,
1457, 1473, 1476, 1578, 1628
Heaven, heavenly xii, 74, 224, 237,
440 469, 515, 648, 779, 783, 785,
923, 1060, 1067, 1111, 1159, 1163,
1202, 1232, 1241, 1279, 1289, 1311,
1421, 1430
Hell 34, 367, 378, 480, 711–712,
783, 923, 1028, 1159, 1192, 1430
Help 30, 58, 252, 290, 434,
583–584, 813, 1213, 1343, 1356
Hero 556
Hide, hidden see Conceal
Holy 157, 221, 393, 702, 735, 896
Home 47, 84, 146, 466, 898, 951,

1567; building 1047; house 438,
    458–459, 1517; mansion 793;
    palace 32; roof 458, 1016
Honesty 200, 660, 943, 1584;
    sincerity 20, 808, 1207, 1211, 1213
Honor 63–64, 456, 460, 486, 640,
    682, 823, 843, 1645
Horse see Animals
House see Home
Human, humanity see Mankind
Humility 486, 569, 811–851, 1592;
    modesty 392, 838–839, 1523
Hurt, hurtful see Harm
Husbands 451–452, 461, 467,
    470

Ignorance, ignores, ignorant 28, 81,
    96, 100, 130, 271, 378, 651, 1053,
    1070, 1075, 1084, 1087, 1252, 1574
Illusion 118, 220, 1605–1606
Immoral 782
Immortality 127, 191, 229, 612, 809,
    901, 1059, 1071, 1187, 1399, 1462,
    1516; eternal 246, 602, 618, 1143,
    1287, 1613; everlasting 376;
    forever 940, 1233; infinite 246;
    permanent 48
Improve see Correct
Infinite see Immortality
Innate 283, 1101, 1490
Intelligence, intellect 284, 614, 905,
    1180; intellectual 288
Intercourse see Fornication

Jealousy see Envy
Joy see Happiness
Judge, judging see Judgment
Judgment 852–875, 906, 967, 1429;
    the judge 610, 655, 854, 865, 869;
    judging 19, 856, 858, 863, 865,
    869, 875, 970
Just 87, 153, 174; the just 888
Justice 605, 853, 855, 861, 864,
    1456, 1608

Karma 1408
Kill 478, 1234, 1568
King 566, 951, 970, 1605
Kingdom 74, 948, 1297, 1311, 1421
Know see Knowledge
Knowledge 25, 52, 81, 265,
    292–293, 414, 423, 444, 488, 494,
    631, 647, 841, 876–905, 993–995,
    1019, 1115, 1142–1143, 1161, 1224,
    1238, 1307, 1388, 1402, 1474, 1550;
    know, knows, knowing 5, 30,
    68, 139, 140, 145, 175, 177, 195,
    205–206, 208, 231, 237, 266–267,
    272, 275, 299, 303, 353, 355,
    360–361, 399, 479, 490, 493, 512,
    603, 634, 645, 652, 732, 815, 835,
    956, 996, 1040, 1066, 1079, 1140,
    1185, 1199, 1229–1230, 1238, 1243,
    1265, 1304–1305, 1311, 1313, 1316,
    1354, 1380, 1428, 1438, 1447–1448,
    1457, 1466, 1472, 1475, 1477, 1498,
    1625

Labor 412, 1282, 1288, 1588, 1593,
    1595, 1597
Language 906–946; converse 542,
    544; speak 71, 230, 413, 423, 500,
    547, 555, 640, 808, 920, 935, 938,
    941, 946, 1090, 1092, 1253, 1312,
    1450, 1453; speech 86, 300, 514,
    618, 621–622, 675, 699, 911, 929–
    930, 932, 936, 942, 1433, 1490;
    talk 824, 841, 939, 1600; voice
    595, 637, 814, 1204, 1219, 1286,
    1509; word xi, xii, xiii, 10, 99,
    102–103, 173, 188, 202, 279, 281,
    413, 438, 510, 605, 618, 642, 646,
    845, 896, 902, 906–910, 912–923,
    937, 980, 1010, 1147, 1150, 1217,
    1235, 1251, 1333, 1450–1451, 1456,
    1492, 1573
Last 694, 1141
Law, rule 159, 175, 776, 956, 966,
    1006
Laziness 129, 1029, 1535; sloth 184,
    496

Lead *see* Leadership
Leader *see* Leadership
Leadership 947–973; lead 77, 113, 191, 271, 276, 384, 438, 598, 950, 957, 960, 1253; leader 954, 969; rule 490, 615, 973–974; ruler 615, 953, 963–964, 967
Learn, learning, learned *see* Education
Liar *see* Lying
Liberality 495
Liberty 731; liberation 229, 625, 1093, 1205, 1229, 1243, 1258
Lie *see* Lying
Life, lifetime 9, 37, 49, 79, 110, 116, 134, 140–141, 144, 152, 214, 229, 236, 251, 271, 326, 376, 418–419, 460, 473, 542, 553, 589, 610, 669, 716, 734, 802, 843, 876, 881, 893, 905, 931, 959, 997, 1013, 1034, 1054, 1097, 1110, 1136, 1152, 1195, 1228, 1247–1248, 1265, 1270, 1358, 1382, 1398, 1411, 1417, 1421, 1489, 1512, 1575, 1602; live 43, 134, 186, 394, 411, 416, 458, 683, 689, 951, 987, 997, 1339, 1343, 1466, 1641; living 126, 642–643, 1251; public life 89
Light xi, xiii, 191, 651, 779, 837, 1109, 1178, 1405, 1489
Lips *see* Body
Liquor *see* Drink
Listen, listening *see* Senses
Live *see* Life
Liver *see* Body
Living *see* Life
Lord *see* God
Lord, master *see* Master
Loss, lost 34, 53, 73, 85, 289, 452, 666, 912, 934, 1125, 1188, 1394, 1512, 1531, 1540, 1581, 1622
Love 31, 106, 225, 262, 265, 272, 285, 295, 370–371, 401, 449, 452, 456–457, 461, 481, 521, 523, 539–540, 550, 553, 555, 606, 619, 623, 659, 663–664, 674, 715, 726, 776, 778, 786, 790, 810, 812, 904, 931, 964, 968, 973–1014, 1035,

1124, 1133, 1152, 1188, 1326, 1343, 1447, 1452, 1475, 1528, 1561, 1574, 1578, 1591, 1598, 1604, 1628, 1630, 1642; affection 1415; cupidity 328, compassion 185, 569, 977
Luck 248, 501
Lust 110, 380, 765, 790, 1015–1039, 1063, 1588
Luxury *see* Wealth
Lying, liar 420, 422, 428, 435, 438, 1399; lie 198, 421, 424, 429, 432

Male 1156, 1484
Man xi, xiii, 51, 54, 62, 66, 68, 71, 88, 108–109, 111–112, 117, 120–121, 125, 130, 135, 144, 160, 192, 194, 200–201, 205, 208, 221, 236, 240–241, 247–248, 251, 254–255, 257–258, 260, 268, 275, 299, 314, 328–329, 360–361, 365, 372, 378, 384, 389, 397–398, 404, 407, 409, 429, 442, 445, 455, 476, 486, 489, 553, 556, 609, 623, 662, 675, 724, 730–731, 748, 751, 760, 765, 785, 791, 796, 797, 825–827, 834, 837, 855, 864, 887, 998, 1022, 1027–1028, 1082, 1088, 1092, 1107, 1131–1132, 1150, 1152, 1159, 1166, 1180, 1195–1196, 1225, 1231–1233, 1235, 1248, 1252, 1290, 1314, 1324, 1330, 1333, 1354, 1385, 1393, 1407, 1417–1418, 1425, 1457, 1470, 1475, 1502, 1526, 1534, 1571, 1582, 1586, 1595, 1604–1605, 1611, 1630; angry man 767; bad man 304, 685, 1242; bad-learned man 1057; blind man 950, 1177–1178; gentleman 57, 60, 70, 96, 188, 347, 357, 552, 584, 690, 817, 927, 1245, 1345; common man 347; considerate man 699; divine man 56; envious man 332; evil man 582; fellow man 869, 1006; foolish man 716, 1379; good man 433, 685, 698, 1242; good-learned man 1057; great man 85,

234, 550, 965; greedy man; 718;
inferior man 63, 67, 354; laboring man 1595; learned man 1551;
little man 1044; malicious
man 871; older man 106; perfect
man 56; pious man 1132;
pleasure-seeking man 1022; poor
man 497; proud man 822; rash
man 716; righteous man 311, 416,
428, 1049, 1203, 1235; sensible
man xii, 102, 493, 1347; small
man 60, 817, 1245, 1345; stingy
man 706, 718; stupid man 491;
superior man 67, 827, 1128;
violent man 316; virtuous
man 1514; wicked man 434; wise
man 30, 61, 99, 173, 234, 311,
506, 558, 766, 774, 882, 936, 949,
1073, 1167, 1182, 1229, 1320, 1416,
1552, 1573; workman 1594
Mankind 338, 1040-1077, 1339,
1355, 1483; evil men 177; great
men 75, 1044, 1569; honest men
660; human 194, 739, 751, 1034;
humanity 975, 1040; men xiii,
65, 99-100, 113, 121, 131, 148, 256,
364, 382, 424, 448, 471, 475, 515,
598, 625, 668, 690, 745, 795, 830,
962, 964, 1007, 1033, 1108, 1111,
1120, 1127, 1136, 1265, 1556, 1596,
1643; superior men 545; virtuous
men 1507
Mansion see Home
Master 254, 283, 307, 975, 1059,
1094, 1189, 1251, 1298; lord 1407,
1511
Medicine 221, 226, 780
Meditation xiii, 30, 1338, 1361,
1442, 1550, 1566
Men see Mankind
Mind 32-33, 54, 93, 149, 160, 194,
199, 203, 227, 289, 299, 308, 481,
494, 619, 652, 714, 743, 750, 1016,
1038, 1061, 1078-1110, 1181, 1231,
1239, 1261, 1318, 1330, 1373, 1432,
1490, 1525, 1562, 1588, 1628
Misery see Grief
Mistake see Error

Moderation 1111-1137;
temperance 106, 1115
Modesty see Humility
Money 370, 715, 744, 1531-1532,
1536, 1541, 1543, 1546
Monk 331
Morals 65, 1264
Mortal, mortality 133, 229, 255,
612, 809, 1462
Mosque see Church
Mother 440, 443-445, 469, 1182,
1555
Mountain see Nature, earth
Mouth see Body
Music 1194, 1578
Mystery 1400, 1577

Nature, earth 1045; earth 440, 648,
711, 779, 824, 1067, 1182, 1197,
1241, 1421, 1483; mountain 785,
1325; rain 963, 1016; rivers 785,
1325, 1638; summer 203, 239; sun
775; wind 61, 721, 1091, 1330;
winter 239
Nature, man's nature 52, 75, 93,
307, 325, 656, 1017, 1025, 1101,
1104, 1227, 1229, 1338, 1444, 1450,
1490
Neighbor 208, 525, 657, 663, 666,
1000, 1223
Night 124, 464, 742, 754
Nothing 9, 37, 50, 143, 183, 227,
289, 377, 412, 489, 591, 599, 633,
690, 894, 1014, 1138-1139, 1144,
1149, 1157, 1161, 1169, 1185, 1190-
1191, 1390, 1418, 1527, 1534, 1603

Obedience, obey 51
Obtain see Gain
Offspring see Children
Old 71, 106, 246, 280, 444, 526,
537-538, 1047
One, unity 1040, 1491-1492,
1495-1496, 1498, 1503-1504, 1646

Opinion 96, 872, 1434
Opportunity 200, 701
Others xii, 11, 70, 86, 108, 182, 184, 269, 271, 301, 303, 310, 315, 318, 320, 341–343, 346–348, 350, 358, 364, 375, 450, 558, 668, 670, 671–672, 674, 677–678, 729, 769, 773, 821, 836, 862, 867, 935, 979, 1042, 1108, 1164, 1181, 1184, 1294–1295, 1343, 1347, 1349, 1353, 1358–1359, 1363, 1367, 1411–1412, 1645; another 94, 117, 307, 337, 356, 514, 656, 673, 828, 847, 1002, 1008, 1076, 1182, 1274, 1342, 1592
Owner *see* Possessions

Pain 38, 53, 217, 226, 237, 310, 498, 555, 671, 678, 769, 890, 989, 1015, 1039, 1053, 1269, 1287, 1424, 1531
Palace *see* Home
Paradise 1220
Paradox 878, 884, 1138–1163
Parents 278, 441–442, 446–447, 739
Passion 125, 1021, 1024, 1026, 1032, 1189, 1285, 1314, 1330, 1388, 1440
Path 107, 112, 171, 384, 673, 947, 965, 1557, 1636, 1644
Patience 403, 976, 1401
Peace 53, 213, 215, 326, 686, 907, 917, 1097, 1196, 1261, 1421, 1452, 1588, 1608
People, person 3, 387, 435, 567, 591, 595, 637, 680, 815, 866, 947, 960, 968–969, 1041, 1230, 1268, 1517
Perception 112, 139, 146, 337, 346, 361, 1164–1184, 1327, 1478
Perfection 605, 1154, 1601; perfect 56, 154, 201, 571, 1151, 1496, 1527, 1570
Permanent *see* Immortality
Piety 6, 833, 1210; pious 1132
Pleasure 38, 53, 109, 226, 365, 567, 769, 864, 890, 946, 1018, 1020,

1022–1023, 1027, 1029, 1031, 1039, 1116, 1122, 1228, 1287, 1424, 1492, 1507, 1520, 1620
Poor 422, 566, 570, 963, 1031, 1112, 1193, 1357, 1535; poverty 113, 1600
Possessions 578, 1185–1199; belongs 28; owner 1104, 1575; possesses 890, 1104, 1161, 1401
Poverty *see* Poor
Power 68, 353, 695, 1262, 1492, 1562, 1605
Praise 61, 68, 815, 828, 949, 1224, 1274, 1570
Pray 356, 518, 525, 659, 1202, 1204, 1208, 1210–1212, 1215, 1221, 1223, 1225
Prayer 153, 1176, 1200–1226, 1273
Pride 58, 88, 110, 120, 423, 813, 818, 820, 825, 835, 850, 1196, 1229, 1232, 1314; egoism 398
Profit 22, 916, 1600
Promise 187, 189
Prophecy, prophets 196, 1173
Prosperity 170, 548, 787, 824, 1350; growth 600
Proverb *see* Sayings
Providence 238
Public life *see* Life
Punishment 294, 420, 1281
Pupil 73, 801
Purity, pure 20, 98, 390, 481, 591, 868, 993, 1082, 1084, 1092, 1109, 1232, 1235, 1238–1239, 1388, 1446, 1587
Purpose 224, 1066, 1264, 1268, 1338, 1341
Pursuit 166, 425, 1033, 1142, 1499, 1546, 1557

Quest 184, 1227–1268

Rain *see* Nature, earth
Rare 49, 194, 427
Rebuke 506, 978, 1012

Receive *see* Reward
Reform *see* Correct
Rejoice *see* Celebration
Relatives *see* Family
Reliance *see* Faith
Religion xiii, 145, 293, 724, 933, 1056, 1456, 1547, 1627, 1630, 1632, 1636, 1643; religionist 759
Respect 76, 90, 106
Revelry *see* Celebration
Reward 165, 216, 294, 704, 1118, 1260, 1269–1292, 1520, 1587; receive 268, 454, 565, 736, 986, 1060, 1185, 1187, 1206
Rich *see* Wealth
Riches *see* Wealth
Right 18, 50, 67, 87, 98, 101, 103, 147, 149, 157, 159, 162, 174, 178, 218, 272, 310, 359, 386, 402, 591, 610, 703, 709, 754, 856, 1049, 1138, 1157, 1290, 1410, 1540, 1642
Righteous 100, 132, 250, 311, 411, 585, 587, 746, 1049, 1209, 1399
Righteousness xi, 152, 274, 936, 1538
Rivers *see* Nature, earth
Roof *see* Home
Root 51, 286, 370–371, 989, 1513
Rule, govern *see* Leadership
Rule, law *see* Law
Ruler *see* Leadership

Sacred xii, 917, 1481, 1588
Sacrifice 87, 250, 1413
Sage 56, 197, 473, 505, 1146
Salvation, save, saved 490, 560–561, 1231, 1237, 1240, 1250, 1252, 1599
Save, saved *see* Salvation
Sayings xii, xiii, 179; proverb xii, 509
Scales, weights 436, 857, 860, 946
Scriptures xi, 199, 288, 353, 431; books xii, 917, 1621
Sea, ocean 372, 798, 1236, 1402, 1638; waves 1330

Secret 23, 559, 1383
Seek 158, 261, 289, 683, 686, 705, 885, 899, 1231, 1244–1245, 1255, 1259–1260, 1262, 1266–1267, 1280, 1478
Self 36, 56, 367, 465, 593, 656, 1009, 1109, 1196, 1227, 1235, 1241, 1293–1313, 1412, 1477, 1500, 1510
Selfishness 183, 319, 330, 716, 1001, 1227, 1409, 1422
Senses 621, 1018, 1083, 1109, 1251, 1314–1338; feel, touch 93, 331, 375, 1152, 1325; hear, listen xii, xiii, 50, 72, 202, 230, 291, 303, 506, 619, 1175, 1310, 1319, 1321–1323, 1325, 1329, 1333, 1335, 1337, 1471, 1552; sound 73, 145, 1316; sight, see 50, 72, 145, 193, 230, 346, 385, 388, 394, 612, 619, 640–641, 649–650, 868, 1146–1147, 1173, 1175, 1316, 1321–1322, 1324–1325, 1327, 1329, 1331, 1333–1335, 1462, 1464, 1503, 1552; smell 1388; taste 1315, 1328, 1388
Sensual, sensuousness 1027, 1029, 1038, 1320
Servant 955
Service 467, 1054, 1339–1358, 1541, 1631
Shadow 259, 1072, 1092
Sheep *see* Animals
Shepherd 959, 1050
Sick *see* Disease
Sight, see *see* Senses
Silver xiii, 198, 725, 920, 1073
Sin, sins 121, 175, 223, 313, 359, 476, 515, 525, 570, 797, 913, 1049, 1085, 1118, 1239, 1359–1385, 1389, 1420, 1544, 1567, 1582, 1586; sinful 219, 925, 1025, 1102; sinner 324, 710
Sincerity *see* Honesty
Sinful *see* Sin
Sinner *see* Sin
Sister 440
Slave 273, 1034, 1189; enslaved 162
Sleep 115, 123, 800, 806, 1132–1133,

1595; dream 204, 1173, 1577;
  drowsiness 1112
Sloth see Laziness
Smell see Senses
Son 51, 277, 445, 462–463, 465,
  536, 951
Sorrow see Suffering
Soul 14, 29, 130, 136, 210, 215, 219,
  449, 478, 529, 544, 563, 658, 681,
  687, 711, 747, 815, 880, 1276, 1355,
  1369, 1385–1407, 1520, 1567, 1612,
  1628
Sound see Senses
Sow 239, 247, 366, 1017
Speak see Language
Speech see Language
Spider see Animals
Spirit 26–27, 37, 50, 82, 127, 652,
  825, 844, 850, 929, 1007, 1025,
  1257, 1640
Spirituality 805, 841, 1013, 1097,
  1234, 1308
Steal 216, 898, 1197; thief 200, 429,
  898, 1197
Steps see Walking
Strength 55, 62, 194, 276, 519, 609,
  818, 1151, 1264, 1554, 1628;
  strong 217, 234, 511, 609, 1004,
  1295; stronger 399
Strong see Strength
Stupid see Foolishness
Success 36, 636, 1246
Suffering 171, 181, 246, 508, 1108,
  1408–1426, 1596; sorrow 64, 127,
  204, 496, 792
Summer see Nature, earth
Sun see Nature, earth

Talk see Language
Task 21, 842, 1589–1590
Taste see Senses
Teach, teaching see Education
Teacher see Education
Temperance see Moderation
Temple see Church
Temptation 66

Theatre 38
Think, thinking see Thought
Thought xi, 10, 78, 92, 95, 625,
  638, 675, 699, 750, 777, 782,
  1032, 1078, 1085, 1090, 1110, 1145,
  1235, 1251, 1254, 1355, 1427–1446,
  1451, 1639, 1643; think, thinking 36, 46, 78, 129, 142, 200, 205,
  240, 499, 502, 622, 629, 688, 851,
  1354
Time 55, 91, 111, 302, 540, 591, 776,
  908, 936, 1287, 1305, 1319, 1394,
  1596
Today see Day
Tomorrow see Day
Tongue see Body
Touch see Senses
Treasure 397, 455, 531, 711, 789,
  893, 898, 946, 1197, 1232, 1623
Trouble 366, 549, 1020, 1069, 1164,
  1184; dangerous 785, 903
Trust 86, 405
Truth xii, 27, 30, 116, 191, 330, 407,
  414, 425, 427, 430, 439, 555, 605,
  612, 617, 634, 644, 734, 941, 991,
  1005, 1010, 1156, 1163, 1216, 1241,
  1253, 1312, 1365, 1447–1481, 1579,
  1608, 1632–1633, 1640; true 56,
  170, 185, 285, 752, 861, 917, 1169,
  1301, 1580; veracity 437

Understand 67, 137, 352, 785, 914,
  947, 1175, 1181, 1185; understanding 109, 155, 290, 314, 363, 405,
  730, 1055
Unity 1484–1502
Universal 942, 1404
Universe 39, 602, 1059, 1081, 1095,
  1388, 1436, 1487

Vain 102, 183, 926, 1013, 1467,
  1615
Vanity 398, 645, 684, 811, 1046
Veracity see Truth

Victory 53, 138, 276, 756, 1480;
  win 443, 452, 1125, 1397, 1581
Virtue 68, 105, 179, 252, 397, 423,
  453, 455, 608, 814, 845, 915, 939,
  1074, 1115, 1228, 1371, 1404,
  1505–1527
Voice see Language

Walking 258, 483, 497, 837, 1256,
  1309, 1471; steps 241, 255, 257,
  1433
War 219; battle 53
Water 544, 550, 741, 796, 1054,
  1402
Waves see Sea
Way 1, 27, 92, 95, 112, 154, 166, 170,
  258, 271, 316, 333, 483, 803, 934,
  1118, 1248, 1256, 1642
Wealth 329, 409, 543, 479, 583,
  715, 793, 826, 843, 1123, 1265,
  1513, 1528–1547, 1576; rich 444,
  952, 1505, 1529, 1533; the rich
  584; riches 59, 720, 733, 1055,
  1103, 1192, 1517, 1520, 1537, 1581
Weep see Grief
Wicked 100, 250, 332, 383, 434,
  585, 660, 784, 1209
Wife, wives 451–452, 454–456, 458,
  460–461, 466, 470, 536, 1182
Will 273, 705, 969, 1232–1233, 1241,
  1423
Wind see Nature, earth
Wine see Drink
Winter see Nature, earth
Wisdom xii, 54, 81, 109, 296, 486,
  488, 609, 652, 730, 818, 820, 985,
  1052, 1224, 1236, 1529, 1548–1581,
  1637
Wise xi, 193, 291, 311, 445, 493, 510,
  535, 609, 722, 913, 1087, 1117,
  1313, 1397, 1563, 1569; the
  wise 72, 134, 161, 502, 511, 724,
  772, 774, 918, 937, 956, 1075,
  1134, 1332, 1629
Wish 1441
Woe 17, 193, 563, 722, 1210, 1391
Woman, women 453, 507, 1035,
  1037, 1074, 1120, 1150, 1152, 1180,
  1385; female 1156, 1484
Word see Language
Work, works 391, 406, 413, 747,
  797, 971, 1068, 1250, 1273, 1275,
  1286–1287, 1573, 1582–1601, 1614,
  1639
World 24, 44, 79, 111, 121, 131, 198,
  214, 225, 246, 357, 371, 443, 448,
  453, 465, 490, 511, 600, 625, 654,
  662, 757, 878, 922, 943, 965, 990,
  997, 1009, 1019, 1030, 1191, 1222,
  1235, 1260, 1268, 1284, 1324, 1341,
  1351, 1381, 1416, 1436, 1451, 1487,
  1514, 1550, 1570, 1576, 1602–
  1624
Worldliness, worldly 81, 226, 790,
  798
Worship 1226, 1601, 1625–1646
Wrath see Hatred
Written 242, 245
Wrong see Error

Yesterday see Day
Youth 76, 444, 1278; young 51, 810